To Peter
With all good wishes

signature

Luke Paul

Luke Paul

Finlay A. J. Macdonald

Shoving Leopard

Shoving Leopard
8 Edina Street 2 F 3
Edinburgh, EH2 5PN
United Kingdom
http://www.shovingleopard.com/

First published in 2012
Text © Finlay A J Macdonald 2012

Cover: Nial Smith Design, 13/4 Annandale Street,
Edinburgh, EH7 4AW
ISBN 978-1-905565-21-4

Introduction

This book has been written against the background of the Church of Scotland debate on Ministry and Same Sex Relationships. In particular it focuses on one of the largest consultation exercises ever undertaken by the Church. This involved sending a detailed questionnaire to the Church's 40,000 elders and 1000 plus ministers to ascertain their views on whether the Church should allow people in same sex relationships to be ministers.

Luke Paul tells the story of how this consultation played out in the life of a typical Scottish parish between October 2010 and May 2011. The great Assembly debates on human sexuality are all a matter of record. Since the mid 1950s, when the question was whether homosexual acts between consenting adults should be de-criminalised, the subject has come up at regular intervals. More recently the General Assembly of 2000 considered the government's proposal to abolish Section 28, a legislative provision which barred teaching about homosexuality in schools. In 2006 the question was whether ministers might be specifically authorised to bless civil partnerships, subject to a provision that no minister should be required to do so against his or her conscience. Then in 2009 the Assembly was faced with an appeal by dissenting members of Aberdeen Presbytery against a decision to induct the Rev Scott Rennie, a minister in a same-sex relationship who, in full knowledge of this fact, had been called by the congregation of Queen's Cross Church in the city. The Assembly's response was to uphold the decision of the Presbytery on the basis that it was procedurally correct but also to make clear that no decisions were being made on the principle of the ordination and induction of people in homosexual relationships. Such decisions should await the findings of a Special Commission set up to look into the whole matter, consult widely and report in 2011.

All of these public debates are accessible through the relevant reports and records of General Assembly proceedings. However, accounts of the church-wide consultation at local level are not so readily available. This is due largely to issues of pastoral confidentiality. It would be highly inappropriate for a minister to publish what had been discussed in the Kirk Session or divulge conversations with parishioners. What I have done, therefore, is to construct what my own experience suggests is a credible account of what might have transpired when a fairly typical minister and congregation engaged with the issues. For the record I would add that I did not myself participate in the consultation at either presbytery or kirk session level.

I have named my fairly typical minister "Luke Paul" because it seems to me that a healthy ministerial formation draws on both evangelist and apostle. Certainly both have their place in this debate. Paul's comments are often quoted on one side of the argument as a sufficient basis for a straightforward condemnation of homosexual acts. Meanwhile, those on the other side set their thinking within a wider context of Gospel grace and acceptance such as is found in St Luke's parables of the Prodigal Son and the Good Samaritan.

The Reverend Luke Paul would much have preferred this debate to have waited until he retired in a few years time. Nevertheless, he is prepared to engage with it, doing so from the perspective of a readiness to accept gay ministers. At the same time he seeks to be respectful of those who take a different view and is deeply troubled at the prospect of a split in the Kirk he has loved and served for nearly 40 years.

My primary reason, then, for writing this book is to set out some kind of record of the debate and its implications at parish level.

My second reason is a hope that church people who read it will hear the differing opinions put forward by elders and others with whom Luke engages, recognise that there is a place for diversity within an underlying Christian unity and think long and hard before leaving the Church, should the ultimate decision be contrary to their own point of view.

A third reason looks beyond the Church's internal debates and divisions. Sadly, it is the case that the Church of Scotland, like most mainline churches is losing members and making a minimal impact upon the rising generation. Of course we must stand up for the Gospel and hold fast to our faith. But so often the perception is that the Church's default stance on many current issues is negative and critical, not least on the questions at the heart of this debate. My hope, therefore, is that those beyond the membership of the Church who read this book may see, not only why this is a difficult question for many Christians, but also perceive something of the grace of the Gospel and those who strive to minister in its name.

Inevitably, what I have written draws on my own experience. This involved ministry in two parishes over a period of 25 years, followed by 14 years as Principal Clerk to the General Assembly, with a year out to serve as Moderator. Accordingly, I have had a ringside seat at Assembly debates of recent years; but I also write from an informed perspective of congregational and parish life. Not all of my ministerial colleagues will agree with Luke Paul's opinions and actions. I do hope, though, that they will identify with the way he seeks to engage seriously with the issue through biblical preaching and pastoral care and perhaps even recognise in him something of themselves.

To avoid cluttering up the text with explanatory and background material to do with the ways of the Church I have prefaced each chapter with a brief note relevant to its content.

While the story is set against the backdrop of real events the main characters are entirely fictional though, I believe, broadly representative of church people. That said, any similarities to real people whose names feature in this story is entirely coincidental.

Finally I would like to express my thanks to the Rev Dr Marjory MacLean and the Very Rev Dr John Miller who read early drafts of the book and whose constructive criticisms have, in my view, much improved the final version. I am also indebted to the Very Rev Dr Alan McDonald, the current Church of Scotland delegate to the General Synod of the Church of England, who read the chapters relating to the Synod to ensure that they fairly portrayed the meeting and decisions of that body. Finally, my thanks to Janet de Vigne of Shoving Leopard for her advice, encouragement and not least, her willingness to allow Luke Paul's thoughts and experiences to be shared with a wider readership.

Finlay A J Macdonald
Candlemas 2012

1

*In 1929 there had been a union between the Church of
Scotland and the United Free Church, the latter representing
the tradition which had left in the Disruption of 1843. By
1956 the membership of the re-united Church of Scotland
had peaked at 1.3 million, compared with 450,000 in 2010.
This was the Church in which Luke grew up as a "son of the
manse."*

Being a minister is not just about singing hymns and
saying prayers.

The Reverend Luke Paul often recalled these words. They
had been spoken by his father when Luke had announced that
he was not continuing with his law studies. Instead he planned
to read theology and enter the ministry. The paternal reaction
had taken Luke by surprise, not least since his father was
himself a minister. True, the ministry had not been his father's
first career choice either. However, his medical studies having
been interrupted by the Second World War, Andrew Paul, like
many of his generation, had responded to a call to ministry
and, on demobilisation, entered Trinity College, Glasgow.
There he had sat at the feet of teachers such as William Barclay,
entering the ministry of the Church of Scotland as the Kirk
headed towards its glory days of the 1950s and 60s.

These were the years of Luke's childhood and youth.
Growing up in Glasgow, where his father secured a parish

appointment, Luke had attended Sunday School, Boys' Brigade and church services without undue protest. After all, many of his friends and their families did the same. The Boys' Brigade Company had over 100 lads aged between 12 and 18 and the local BB "hut" was a cool place to hang out, not just on Friday parade evenings but every night of the week. Classes leading to badges were offered on subjects such as first aid, map reading, camping skills, gymnastics and Scripture knowledge. After class there was snooker and table tennis and, if the pocket money stretched, the walk home could be accompanied by tuppence worth of chips. An extra penny would allow for mushy peas on the side. On Sunday morning there was BB Bible Class at 9am. It was a proud boast of Luke's company that they met at 9 am – not like other (lazy) companies which held Bible Class at 10. Old Jim Wilson, one of the senior officers, wheezed away on the harmonium to accompany Moody and Sankey hymns. Luke's best pal was Danny, who fairly burst with pride when the captain announced the hymn "Dare to be a Daniel":

> *Dare to be a Daniel; dare to stand alone;*
> *Dare to have a purpose true; dare to make it known.*

Then there was summer camp - 100 boys, officers, cooks (officers' wives), not forgetting the piano to accompany morning and evening worship. The camp site at Gartocharn on the eastern shores of Loch Lomond was laid out with military precision, most of the older officers having seen active war service – one or two in the First World War- and the younger ones recently returned from national service. An elevated, wooded piece of land close to the camp was known as "Hill 60" having been so named in the 1920s by officers who had survived the trenches. There were bell tents for the boys, square bell tents for the officers and marquees for the canteen, stores and tuck shop. Reveille was sounded at 7am with tent and kit inspection taking place before breakfast.

Such memories contributed to what Luke readily acknowledged was a happy childhood. Now, nearing retirement and thinking back to those far off days, he could not but contrast the life of a typical congregation then and now. Those were the days of post-war reconstruction with new council housing developments in Scotland's cities and the creation of whole new towns such as Irvine, Livingston, Cumbernauld, Glenrothes and East Kilbride.

As a student Luke had become involved in one of these new church extension charges, as they were called. The new "housing scheme" had been built on the edge of his father's parish and, in his late teens, encouraged by his father, he had thrown in his lot with the new congregation. The parish was bustling with life, the congregation full of families revelling in the move from sub-standard tenements, with shared outside toilets, to semi-detached and terraced homes with bathrooms and gardens. In the midst of the community a brand new church building with generous hall accommodation offered a range of activities for all age groups and went like a fair seven days a week. Luke and the minister's son, Iain, started a Saturday evening youth club which was hugely popular with local teenagers. Only once did things get out of hand when a fight broke out. As a consequence of trying to separate the feuding clans Luke and Iain ended up in the casualty department of the Royal Infirmary. Their cuts and bruises soon healed but there had been some damage to furniture and furnishings. As a consequence the Youth Club was put on notice by the Kirk Session – but it survived.

Luke also became involved with something called the "Scottish Churches' Student Team" – a group of enthusiastic and idealistic individuals drawn from different denominations and universities who spent the last fortnight of September in a church extension parish. They camped in the church halls, assisted with youth work and knocked on doors throughout the community with invitations to become involved in the life of the new local church. Many did, finding a fresh lease of spiritual as well as domestic life in their new surroundings. Undeniably his association with such a heady mix of spiritual energy, infectious enthusiasm and sheer optimism was a major factor in Luke's decision to switch courses and study for the ministry. Why then the old man's rather curious response – "Being a minister is not just about singing hymns and saying prayers"?

Luke's father, the Reverend Andrew Paul, was extremely well read and, as was the ministerial fashion of his day, adorned his sermons with a ready supply of apt quotations and pithy aphorisms. His family would also 'benefit' from these if father thought the occasion appropriate. Longfellow was a great favourite and the protestant work ethic was readily inculcated when, for example, homework was given second place to the latest episode of Z cars:

*The heights by great men reached and kept
Were not attained by sudden flight;
But they, while their companions slept,
Were toiling upward in the night.*

or:

*Lives of great men all remind us
We can make our life sublime
And departing leave behind us
Footprints on the sands of time.*

If accused of inconsistency Emerson came readily to hand: *A foolish consistency is the hobgoblin of little minds*; and if charged with double standards Douglas Bader was quickly cited as witness for the defence: *Rules are for the obedience of fools and the guidance of wise men.* Rev Andrew could also mint his own *mot juste* when the occasion called for it. A lippy parishioner, who once remarked that she was sure she had heard the sermon before, received the response: *If you remember a sermon it was clearly worth repeating and if you don't it's time you heard it again.* Not able to find this in the *Oxford Dictionary of Quotations*, which was never far from his father's desk, Luke assumed that the warning that ministry was not just about singing hymns and saying prayers came from the same homespun source.

Around twenty years before Luke's father had been ordained there had been a major church union in Scotland which brought together the United Free Church and the Church of Scotland. As both were presbyterian churches this made a lot of sense but, right from the start, it was recognised that if union made sense at national level it also made sense at congregational level. In other words, as opportunities arose – usually when a minister retired or died – neighbouring congregations should unite and fill one building instead of half-filling two. This was the theory but in practice it didn't always work out in a straightforward way. Inevitably different customs existed in the congregations being asked to unite. In one the offering was taken up during the service, in the other arriving members placed their offering in an alms dish at the door; in one they used the "debts" form of the Lord's Prayer, while in the other they said "trespasses"; for Holy Communion one congregation would use the common cup and a decent port wine while the other favoured individual glasses and non-alcoholic wine. Pity then the poor minister who had to try to weld into one united congregation a group of strong-minded individuals who regarded their way of doing things, not only as non-negotiable, but as being of the very essence of the Kingdom of God. As if this wasn't challenging enough there was the further question of which set of buildings to retain and which to dispose of.

On the retirement of the long serving and much loved minister of the neighbouring congregation Andrew Paul became one such minister towards the end of the 1950s. It was clear from the start that neither group of elders was going to give up their cherished traditions without a fight. Mercifully the choice of buildings was fairly easily settled as only one of the churches was on a site that would allow for commercial development. However, that meant that there was money available and that, in turn, meant that decisions had to be taken as to how these funds should be used. One of the church buildings was indeed sold to a developer while one of the manses was sold on the open market and fetched a good price. The plan was to invest part of this "windfall" and to use the rest to upgrade the church buildings - church, hall and manse - which were retained. This created even more opportunities for argument over how much to invest and how much to spend, followed by further disagreement about how to spend the proportion which was not to be invested. One hope the Paul family secretly harboured was that funds might be made available to install central heating in the large, draughty manse in which they were to remain. No such luck and Andrew would not have dreamed of pressing his own interest; but, at least, this was one matter on which everyone else was agreed.

As he thought of this Luke recalled a line from one of Garrison Keillor's Lake Woebegone tales. In order to help balance the church budget the local Lutheran pastor had offered to forego attendance by himself and his wife at a clergy conference to be held in Florida the following January. The offer was gratefully accepted by the Board of Deacons. When the pastor returned home that night and informed his wife that they would not after all be leaving the Minnesotan winter for ten days in the sunshine state she was not best pleased and remarked: "Honey, the first martyrs went to their martyrdom alone; they didn't take their wives along with them."

Like many a colleague seeking to form a genuine union of two congregations Luke's father persisted with what St Paul called "the ministry of reconciliation" and did so with some degree of success. Through a mixture of patience, assiduous pastoral care, thoughtful preaching and sympathetic conduct of funerals many were won over. Luke's mother, Aileen, also played her part as the "traditional minister's wife," running the Woman's Guild, answering the manse telephone and maintaining a list of birthdays of church members aged 80 and over (a significant age in those days) so that they would receive a birthday greeting from the Church.

Looking back on that period Luke could well understand his father's disappointment and frustration. Having emerged from the war with a sense of high calling, a desire to help shape the moral and spiritual values of the nation and contribute to a better world order, here he was reduced to refereeing petty squabbles between strong-willed individuals within what was meant to be the body of Christ. Perhaps this explained his father's cautionary counsel when Luke intimated his decision to follow him into the ministry: "Being a minister is not just about singing hymns and saying prayers."

2

Luke and his father might both be described as "Auld Kirk Moderates." The term dates back to the eighteenth century when one effect of the Scottish Enlightenment was to divide ministers into two parties known as Moderates and Evangelicals. The former tended to embrace the new thinking; the latter were more cautious in face of anything which might appear to challenge traditional Christian teaching.

These musings on his early years accompanied Luke on a morning walk through his beloved Pentland Hills. Later that day he would have to chair a meeting of his Kirk Session especially called to consider a consultation paper from the General Assembly on the ministry and same sex relationships. And he was not looking forward to this. It was one of those glorious autumn days which had begun with a touch of frost, but by mid morning a warming sun was shining in a clear blue sky. The only clouds were those in prospect that evening. He had never been good with conflict.

Luke's father had long since been "translated to higher service" (to use a favourite Kirk euphemism for dying). Luke himself was now approaching forty years in the ministry and had had moments in three charges when, if one of his own children had announced a desire to enter the ministry he might well have repeated his father's health warning. In the event daughter Anne had followed her mother, Joyce, into teaching while their son Richard had become an accountant. Luke did observe wryly, however, that when Anne announced her interest in teaching her mother had not been overly enthusiastic. But it pleased him that both Anne and Richard were involved in their local churches – one in Argyll, the other in Fife – and that his grandchildren had been baptised and attended Sunday School. Richard even served as treasurer in his congregation. He had never mentioned the 'issue of the moment' but Anne had once declared that she just couldn't understand the 'stushie' (her word) created by the 2009 General Assembly's decision to allow a gay minister in a civil partnership to be inducted as minister of a congregation and parish. "Good luck to him and to them," she had said, adding for good measure: "I thought the Church of Scotland believed in congregations having the right to choose their own ministers."

"Would that it were so simple," Luke mused as he powered up Howden Glen towards the shoulder of Allermuir Hill. He loved this walk, pausing every so often to survey the view afforded by another hundred feet of elevation. He watched a plane coming into land at Edinburgh Airport and gazed at the city spread out before him. There was the castle, the spires of St Mary's Cathedral to the left, the crown of St. Giles' to the right; there was Arthur's Seat and beyond the city the River Forth and the Lomond Hills providing a dramatic backdrop to the Rosyth Ferry nearing the end of its voyage from Zeebrugge. What tales this city could tell – stories of Mary Queen of Scots, John Knox and the Scottish Reformation the

450th anniversary of which was being marked this very year; tales of the Scottish Enlightenment and men such as Adam Smith, Robert Adam and David Hume, the tercentenary of whose birth would be marked next year. Long before the concept of European City of Culture had been thought of, thanks to men such as these Edinburgh had been proclaimed 'the Athens of the North'. Luke had studied Hume as part of an undergraduate philosophy course and remained a fan of "the Great Infidel" as James Boswell affectionately nicknamed him.

By now the steep path up the glen had levelled out and Luke had a choice. He could veer east and strike up to the summit of Allermuir, thence along the ridge towards Caerketton, down to Swanston Village, then work his way back to the car park off the by-pass at Dreghorn; or he could turn west, descending gradually towards Bonaly. He chose the former route. It was a clear day and the view from Allermuir Hill would stretch to the Sidlaw Hills beyond Dundee and to the high Munros of Stirlingshire and Perthshire, the whole splendid panorama framed by Ben Lomond in the west and the Bass Rock in the east. On a more mundane level this route had the added option of a bowl of soup at Swanston Golf Club on the way back to the car. He would be ready for that.

He needed to clear his head before this evening's meeting which he feared would be difficult. He required to think through what he would say himself, but also how to encourage those who would be hesitant about speaking. At the same time it would be important to ensure that more forceful elders did not dominate the proceedings. What was it about this issue, he asked himself, which had the potential to be so bitterly divisive?

Luke found himself thinking that had he been living in the age of David Hume and Adam Smith he would have thrown in his lot with the Moderates rather than the Evangelicals. He liked to think that he was open to new ideas as the Moderates had been. They had embraced the spirit of the Enlightenment and began to look again at some of their doctrinal stances such as predestination. This taught that from the beginning some were predestined to everlasting glory (the elect) while others (the damned) were doomed to everlasting torment. Who really believed that today, Luke wondered. Robert Burns "Holy Willie's Prayer" came to mind where the poet lampoons the paragon of self-righteousness who takes equal delight in the doom of the damned as in his own self-assured salvation.

Luke recalled from his church history studies how Enlightenment ideas even led some to question Church teaching that salvation can be found in Christ alone. How could it be, people asked, that a loving, creator God could sanction eternal torment to the millions of people throughout the world who had never even heard of Christ? In time yet further questions arose over the literal meaning of Scripture. When Genesis talked of God creating the world in six days did it really mean what we understand today by Sunday to Friday? The Moderates were prepared to ask these questions. The Evangelicals, while also educated men of great intellectual power, were more cautious, less trustful of where entirely rational thought might lead and content to place their faith squarely in Christ as revealed in Scripture. Again

Luke returned to the thought that the present divisions over attitudes to homosexuality were no more than a 21st century equivalent of these earlier controversies.

By now Luke had reached the summit of Allermuir Hill where he sat for a while watching the traffic bustling along the Edinburgh city by-pass. Everyone is in such a rush, he thought, recalling W.H, Davies' famous lines: "What is this life if full of care/we have no time to stand and stare?" Certainly the view from the top merited a stare and was well worth the effort of the climb. To the north, far beyond the city and the river rose the rugged mountains of the central highlands; southwards stretched the undulating Pentland range and gentler Border hills. Psalm 121 came readily to mind: "I will lift up mine eyes unto the hills...."

As he sat by the trig point munching an apple Luke's reminiscences returned to his own early life. His father's congregation had been called St Luke's and that explained Luke's own name. He had two older sisters, Eleanor who was seven when Luke had been born and Judith who had been five. Eleanor recalled a ripple of amusement the day their baby brother had been baptised 'Luke' by their father's old college friend, the Reverend Graeme Douglas. The cynic might have wondered if this was the equivalent of a politician currying favour with his constituents in order to gain their support; but that was not particularly the old man's style. In fact the reason was entirely different. When asked, he explained that the boy had been named after Luke the evangelist, author of his favourite Gospel. This had the added benefit, he added wryly, of balancing the non-negotiable surname, 'Paul'.

Certainly, Luke's memory of his father's ministry, reinforced by some father/son theological sparring during his student days, was that Andrew Paul held out the life and ministry of Jesus as narrated in the four Gospels as a model for his flock. He was also a great admirer of St Luke's second volume, *The Acts of the Apostles*, with its action-packed account of the beginnings of the Christian Church. While not entirely ignoring the more doctrinally focussed epistles of Paul he preached on these less frequently. When he did he favoured such inspired passages as 1st Corinthians 13 with its hymn to faith, hope and love and Romans 8, with its assertion that if God is for us who can be against us. His basic difficulty with Paul was the way he seemed to intrude his own opinion on matters such as the role of women in the Church. Perhaps, Luke conjectured, his father had been influenced by his own mother, a feisty highland lady who had been a strong supporter of the suffragette movement. As a boy in the 1950s Luke could recall his grandmother arguing in support of the ministry being opened up to women. "Women were the first apostles of the resurrection," she would insist.

Luke particularly recalled one conversation over a dram in his father's study. The old man was arguing that Luke's Gospel was the most inclusive of the four. He pointed out that only Luke recorded the parables of the Good Samaritan and the Prodigal Son. The point of the former was to show that, while people of the same tribe as the injured man passed by on the other side, one who came from a different tribe stopped and provided help. The clear message was that there is no limit to the concept of neighbour. This meant that no-one should be thought of as being beyond the pale of God's and therefore the Church's care and concern. In the parable of the Prodigal Son it was difficult not to have sympathy for the elder brother. It was also natural to feel that the younger son received no more than his just deserts. Nevertheless he was received back into the family, alongside the loyal and dutiful older son. In Rev Andrew's view this act of grace illustrated God's accepting love and challenged those within the church who were tempted to judge others by a harsher standard than they would wish to be judged themselves.

"Why should that conversation come back to me today, of all days?" wondered Luke.

The reality was that Luke shared his father's love of the Gospels and was proud to be called Luke. At the same time he took pride in his surname and was more than ready to applaud the energy which the apostle Paul had devoted to building up the early Church. He liked the way Paul had challenged Peter's insistence that Gentile converts to Christianity should first undergo Jewish rites such as circumcision. That seemed an unhelpful obstacle to converting people to Christ and bringing them into the life of the Church. However, there was no getting away from the fact that some of Paul's writings were used as a basis for discrimination. He was regularly quoted by those who resisted women's ordination and those who now opposed the acceptance of homosexual ministers.

But now it was time to head down to Swanston for that tempting bowl of soup. Looking back and continuing on the "Luke/Paul" theme he supposed he had been quite 'hard line' on a number of issues during his student and early ministry days. He blushed inwardly as he recalled a student debate in which he had argued strongly against the ordination of women. However, exposure to so many pastoral encounters over the years, not to mention his own life experiences, had undeniably shaped his own faith and theology into a more liberal and tolerant mode. Was it the case, he reflected, that he had started out more Paul than Luke and would soon be retiring more Luke than Paul?

3

In 1966 the General Assembly, following years of discussion throughout the Church, agreed that women were eligible to become elders on the same terms as men. Two years later equivalent legislation opened the ministry to women.

Luke had begun his ministry in the early 1970s. His first parish was centred on the pleasant Highland village of Glenburn. The community had expanded significantly over the previous decade and contained a mix of families and age groups. Some – the real Glenburnians as they liked to call themselves - had lived there for generations; others had come in from different parts of the country, attracted by new housing and a manageable commute to Inverness. Luke had been somewhat taken aback when asked by a member of the Vacancy Committee if he was teetotal. He replied truthfully that he was not and was duly appointed, though not, he trusted, solely on account of that answer. The parish contained a number of distilleries. These produced quality Highland malts which were savoured around the world and made a vital contribution to the local and national economies. What lay behind the question, Luke discovered, was that some years previously the congregation had been served by a minister who was not only teetotal but felt the need to preach every so often on the evils of drink.

A few months after Luke took up his appointment the annual Church Christmas Fayre came round. Now, the official policy of the Church of Scotland has long been to oppose all games of chance and many a minister, anxious to uphold this policy, has come to grief when venturing to ban fund raising initiatives such as guessing the number of sweeties in the jar at the Brownie Coffee Morning. This was presumably why no-one had checked that Luke had no objection to the tradition of a tombola stall, with the main prizes generously gifted by the local distillery. Whether it was discretion being the better part of valour, a case of choosing your battles, or simply needing time to consider where this came on the scale of drinking and gambling, Luke decided just to let things go. After all, these were decent people giving generously of their time and energy to raise money for a good cause. Such matters of principle now seemed less straightforward than when discussed in Divinity College.

In any case there were bigger issues to deal with. It was less than ten years since the Church of Scotland had agreed that women were eligible to be ordained as elders. The Kirk Session to which he had come was all male, but there were a number of women on the Congregational Board, a body to which members of the congregation were elected for three year terms and which had responsibility for financial and property matters. It was clear to Luke that the Session could do with some fresh blood. Having by then overcome his student misgivings he was prepared to argue strongly that the new intake should include some women.

Over recent years he had paid particular attention to the way his father operated and so understood the value of consultation. He proposed that at the next Session meeting the elders should have a discussion on the subject of bringing on some new elders some of whom might be women. The discussion went better than he had feared. There were inevitably those who thought that the time wasn't ripe and that the congregation wasn't ready for such an innovation. There was some concern about what women elders would wear when serving communion. And some expressed the view that none of the women in the congregation would wish to be an elder, this having been regarded for so long as a distinctively male preserve. On the other hand there were those who argued that it was important to move with the times, that there were a number of people who had moved into the village who had been elders in their previous parishes and, as the congregation was growing, it was important to have a few more elders with new ideas. And so a small committee was formed to take the matter forward and less than a year after his induction Luke presided over a service of ordination of six new elders - three men and three women.

To Luke, now driving back home from his Pentland walk and cheered by a bowl of Swanston soup, that all seemed so innocent and so long ago. The Church of Scotland was now embroiled in a much bigger controversy which was set to come to a head at the 2011 General Assembly and he had learned just the other day that he was likely to be a commissioner to that Assembly. He had remained in Glenburn for six years and then moved to the large and busy suburban congregation of St Fillan's, Dundee. After twenty-four years there he had moved south to the smaller charge of Capelaw, just outside Edinburgh from where he was due to retire in two years' time. "Could this not have waited until then?" he fretted.

Luke frequently wondered why the Church had such a hang up with sex. Was it really the most important thing in a relationship? Of course there were serious issues of sexual exploitation, trafficking for the sex trade, rape, paedophilia, casual, unprotected and often alcohol-fuelled sex which resulted in disease, unwanted pregnancies and no end of grief. It was absolutely right that the Church should be in the forefront of challenging a culture which fostered such things and providing support to its victims. But some of his colleagues refused point blank to marry couples who were living together before marriage. To Luke's mind such a domestic arrangement was hardly in the same league and the harsh attitude of judgmental colleagues simply betrayed a prurient obsession with one aspect of a loving relationship to the exclusion of all others. It also seemed to him utterly illogical. If a minister took the view that a man and a woman living together outside marriage was sinful then should such a minister not rejoice when the couple came seeking Christian marriage? But now the big sex related issue was ministry and same sex relationships and that evening Luke's Kirk Session would meet to discuss the matter.

Luke ran his mind over various General Assembly debates on the matter which he had either attended or read about. He recalled being at a General Assembly in the early 1990s (1993 he thought) when there was a row over the fact that a minister had blessed a same sex relationship. This was long before the days of civil partnerships and, inevitably the minister's action had received considerable publicity When the General Assembly came round someone moved that an instruction be issued that no minister should ever do such a thing again. The Assembly, wisely in Luke's view, refused to make such an order, largely on the grounds that it did not consider it appropriate to fetter a minister's freedom to make pastoral judgements. In any event if any concerns were raised about a minister's conduct the proper body to deal with it was the local presbytery.

Luke had also been a commissioner to the General Assembly of 2006 when a controversial proposal had been brought forward by the Legal Questions Committee, not a body particularly known for rocking the boat. Civil partnerships were by then in existence and there had been a number of cases where church members had entered into such partnerships and then sought a blessing from their minister. This placed the minister in an awkward position because it was not entirely clear whether to give such a blessing might leave the minister open to a disciplinary charge. The Committee's idea was to have the Assembly adopt permissive legislation which authorised ministers to agree to such requests if their conscience allowed them to. It also made clear that no minister should be required to provide such a ceremony of blessing if that went against his or her conscience.

Luke thought this was a good proposal and actually spoke in favour of it. His argument was that the Church had a strong tradition of protecting a minister's conscience. He mentioned how the legislation allowing ministers to solemnise marriages involving divorcees specifically provided an opt out for those ministers who could not in all conscience do so. He fully supported the right of ministers not to be required to bless civil partnerships; but he equally supported the right of those who were comfortable with the idea to be able to do so without fear of discipline.

Luke was a minister in Dundee at the time and his speech was reported in the local *Courier* newspaper. This caused him some grief when he returned home. Not all the members of his congregation were pleased to see their minister's name in the paper expressing such opinions. As a consequence a small number decided to move to other congregations where the minister's views were more to their liking. This troubled Luke but he took comfort from the fact that they had not left the Church altogether. After all the Church of Scotland claimed to be a "broad church" and one of the things that particularly distressed Luke was the prospect of a significant split in the Church over the issue.

But now matters had moved on. Luke, too, had moved on and was settled in a smaller though still busy charge for the final years of his ministry. How would the good folk of Capelaw respond to the more sharply focussed question which confronted the Church? The stakes had been raised and what was up for discussion now was not what a minister may or may not do but who may or may not be a minister. The decision of the 2009 General Assembly to allow the induction to a charge of a minister in a same-sex relationship was, Luke surmised, a "game changing" decision, even though it had been made clear that this was not a decision in principle but simply a recognition that those involved in the appointment had acted in good faith and in accordance with the rules at the time. Now, before moving on to consider the question of principle, the Assembly wished to know the views of presbyteries and kirk sessions. To this end a Special Commission, chaired by a serving judge had been appointed to look at all the issues, consult widely and report in 2011. To allow the Commission to get on with its work the Assembly further instructed ministers and church members not to engage in public debate on the matter until the Commission reported. However, discussion within church meetings was encouraged and, in order to assist this, the Commission had issued a consultation document. This asked individual ministers and elders to respond to a range of questions. For example, did they consider homosexuality to be a 'disorder' or a 'given'? Would they accept orientation as a given but disapprove of practice? Would they accept that the Christian concept of marriage might be extended to exclusive, committed same-sex relationships which were intended to be life long? Should someone in a same sex relationship be allowed to be a minister? If the Church allowed/forbad people in a same sex relationship to be a minister would they leave the Church? It was questions such as these which would form the agenda of the evening's Session meeting.

4

The Kirk Session is the governing body of the local congregation. The minister normally acts as moderator or chair of the meeting. Elders also have a pastoral role with the congregation divided into elders' districts. The expectation is that elders maintain regular contact with the people in their district. Once appointed to the Session there is no set time limit on length of service.

There was a good attendance at the Kirk Session with eighteen out of a possible twenty elders present. Luke opened the meeting with a prayer and then gave some background. He pointed out the texts in Leviticus, Romans, 1st Corinthians, 1st Timothy and Jude which condemned homosexuality out of hand and referred also to the strong biblical tradition which commends marriage between a man and a woman as the proper context for sexual relations. This was the 'traditionalist' view. He then pointed out that the position of the Church of Scotland was that the Word of God was 'contained' in the Scriptures of the Old and New Testaments. Some understood this to mean that every word in the Bible was the unerring and unchangeable word of God. Others, by contrast, took the view that the Bible contained both timeless truths and material which was of its time and reflected the values of ancient Israel or the first century Graeco-Roman world. Those who favoured the 'revisionist' view noted that today we have a much greater understanding of the human psyche than people did in biblical times and argued the need to take account of that. They suggested that what the Bible was condemning was licentious and orgiastic conduct, something very different from what we know today as same-sex relationships based on a life-long commitment. Luke stressed that there was place for both views of Scripture within the Church of Scotland.

Luke's worry had been that some of the elders would be reluctant to speak. He knew that at least two of them had grown up children who were gay. Neither had found that easy but he admired the way in which they had come to terms with the situation rather than lose contact with their children. How, he wondered, would they react to the strong opinions some of their fellow elders were quite capable of expressing?

In these situations a classic diversionary technique is to raise a point of order. Luke wondered if this was peculiar to churches in general or just the Church of Scotland. Right on cue Peter Henderson, one of the senior elders who had once represented the Session at the General Assembly, asked why, after the discussion, each individual was to tick the boxes on their consultation paper in private. "Surely, he argued, "we should all be prepared to say openly what we believe. I am quite clear in my own mind that the Bible is the Word of God and that as elders of the Church we should uphold its teaching in word and deed. And I ask you, Moderator, to rule accordingly."

Before Luke could respond Jimmy Souter, who golfed regularly with Peter (was this a set-up, Luke thought to himself) stated that he objected to the procedure which called for the individual returns to be sent to the Special Commission, albeit anonymously, so that a central tally could be made of responses of all the elders of the Kirk to each question.

"What is your problem with this approach, Jimmy?" Luke enquired. "People usually complain about not having had their opinion sought." Jimmy explained: "Surely all we need to send in is the opinion of the Kirk Session expressed in the usual way by taking a vote. I move that this Kirk Session states its complete opposition to sexually active homosexual people becoming ministers." "I second that," interjected Peter, adding for good measure: "This is just another example of the Church trying to be all things to all men. No wonder fewer and fewer people take us seriously."

From the chair Luke was quite firm in ruling the motion out of order. He pointed out that the instructions from the Assembly Commission were very clear. They wanted every one of the Kirk's 40,000 elders to have the opportunity of thinking through the issues and expressing an opinion. This, then, was how they would proceed. The two objectors expressed their annoyance but Luke was encouraged by the sight of several heads nodding in quiet agreement with his ruling. At the same time he knew he had made two powerful enemies who had the capacity to make things difficult for him over the remainder of his ministry.

It was clear that this exchange had unnerved people and Luke had to work hard to encourage others to speak. Eventually Mary White, who Luke knew had a daughter who had recently entered a civil partnership, spoke up. She didn't think it was enough just to quote verses from certain books of the Bible. There were other texts which said things about not judging others, loving your neighbour as yourself, and treating other people the way you would like them to treat you. Having read the material she was more than ever convinced that a person's sexual orientation was something they were born with. She then went on to make what Luke thought was a particularly compelling point. She had been born heterosexual and was happily married with three grown up children. How, she asked her fellow elders, did they think she would have felt if she had come under social or religious pressure to deny her heterosexuality and enter into a homosexual relationship? How would they have felt if they found themselves in such a situation? Would they not have been appalled? Yet, she argued, was this not the very pressure homosexual people came under – to pretend to be something they were not? "It's all very well," she continued, "to say 'love the sinner, hate the sin' but who are we to judge and to call what is a basic element in an individual's make up sin? Did Jesus not say to the crowd about to stone a woman caught in adultery 'Let the one who is without sin cast the first stone.'?"

This gave others confidence to speak. Steve Mitchell, a recent addition to the Session and a maths teacher in one of Edinburgh's private schools, argued that we should not ignore new insights derived from psychology and biology. We knew so much more about our human make up in the twenty-first century than people did in biblical times. At this point Neil Jeffrey, a heating engineer with Scottish Gas, suggested that we should distinguish between orientation and practice. He was prepared to accept that a person could be born homosexual and would have no difficulty with such a person becoming a minister, provided he or she was celibate.

"But is that fair?" interjected Maggie Russell, owner of the florist shop in the High Street: "We wouldn't impose such a requirement on a heterosexual person who at least has the option of marriage and sexual fulfilment. Surely we should apply the same standards to both homosexual and heterosexual persons, namely, that they should not be promiscuous but express their sexuality within an exclusive, committed loving relationship. On this basis," Maggie continued, "I would have no difficulty with a homosexual minister living in a civil partnership. Indeed, is there not a real risk that forcing someone to suppress such a natural element as the sexual drive would lead simply to that drive expressing itself in inappropriate and dangerous ways?"

"That's all very well," interposed Bob McEwan, retired joiner and church property convener, "But I just don't think the Church is ready for a same-sex couple living in the manse. I agree that we should be much less judgmental than we have been in the past but ministers are in a different category and should set an example to the community. And what if the minister and his or her partner wanted to have a family? Gay couples are allowed to adopt now. The Catholic Church fought long and hard to have its adoption agencies exempt from having to go down that road and lost. Or maybe the gay manse couple would want their own child through a surrogacy or sperm donor arrangement. Once we start unpicking the Bible and choosing which bits we need to follow and which bits we can ignore, where will it end?" This sentiment earned a few nods of agreement from some who had not yet spoken and who, Luke surmised, were unlikely to contribute to debate.

These comments were followed by a maiden speech from Matthew Wallace, a post-graduate student at Heriot Watt University, who had recently been appointed to the Session, partly with a view to lowering the average age but, more importantly, to bring a younger person's perspective to discussion. He began: "I notice that one of the questions asks whether you would leave the Church of Scotland if the final decision is one you don't like. I suppose," he continued, "there will be those who see this as such a fundamental issue that it could undermine the Church's whole credibility. Those on one side will argue that to allow sexually active gay ministers would be to embrace heresy. Those on the other side will argue that to refuse would be to endorse and even encourage homophobia, which would run totally against the spirit of the Gospel. For myself I am not persuaded by the arguments I have heard in favour, but if that's the way the decision goes then I won't leave the Church. I won't be too happy but I don't believe this issue is so fundamental that such a decision would destroy the Church's legitimacy or take away from the good work the Church does in communities like ours around Scotland. Indeed, I worry that this whole debate is a distraction from that work. Be that as it may, whatever the outcome, I'll be staying."

After this contribution, which was received with sage nods and murmurs indicating a mix of assent and uncertainty, Jimmy Souter, who had wanted the Session simply to record its opposition to the whole idea of gay clergy, asked Luke what he thought. After all he too had been asked to complete a questionnaire at Presbytery. Luke had anticipated that this might happen. On the one hand he was hesitant about taking a lead in the debate. He wanted people to be free to express their opinions. At the same time he recognised that it was a fair question. After all, part of his function was to instruct people in the faith. The difficulty with this particular issue, though, was that there was a clear division of opinion within the Church as to what the proper Christian approach was.

Luke explained all of this but decided to go on and say that, with the greatest of respect, he did not see the matter in the same clear cut way as those who had spoken first in the discussion. He strongly believed that the Bible contained the eternal truth of God's Word but considered that it also reflected the views of those who had written its chapters over the centuries and the age in which they had lived. He believed that God was still revealing the mysteries of the universe and that we should be grateful for new discoveries such as those which enabled cruel diseases to be cured. He suggested that the Church did not have a particularly good record in embracing new ideas, often seeing them as threatening - for example the persecution of Galileo who taught that the earth went round the sun and fell victim to the Inquisition. Luke went on to state his view that homosexual people had not been well treated in our society, having been criminalised up to the 1960s and the Church had given moral cover to such discrimination. Was there a danger that this remained the case today when homophobia was still at the root of some horrendous hate crimes? He realised how difficult this was for the Church and recognised the fine ministries exercised by colleagues who took an entirely literal view of Scripture. He also acknowledged the sincerity with which differing views were held within the Kirk Session and hoped that they could continue to work together for the good of their church and community. This was a huge issue. He had heard the differing views which had been expressed and was grateful for the candour and sincerity with which the various contributions had been made. Not surprisingly there was disagreement but as church elders there was much more about which members of the Session agreed and he hoped that everyone could focus on that.

As this statement appeared to close down the debate Luke invited the elders to take time to tick the various boxes on the questionnaire. He stressed that there was no need to put their names on the forms and that once they were completed they should hand them to Brian MacFarlane, the Session Clerk, as they left. He thanked all those who had spoken and closed the meeting with a prayer.

5

For many ministers chairing the regular meeting of the Kirk Session is one of their more stressful duties. Chairing such a significant and controversial meeting as this would inevitably take its toll. Luke would be glad to get home and unwind.

"How did it go?" Joyce enquired when Luke arrived home that evening.

"Better than I had feared," he replied. "Various views were expressed but I sensed that nobody was afraid to speak out and that pleased me. I think I have made a couple of enemies, though" – and Luke went on to explain his ruling on the point of order.

"Hello, Dad."

Luke had forgotten that their daughter Anne was staying overnight. She was on a General Teaching Council Committee which was meeting in Edinburgh the next morning and usually travelled down from Argyll the evening before. Otherwise it would have meant a ridiculously early start in the morning.

She continued: "Is this you still fretting over gay ministers? What is the Church's problem? I have colleagues and friends who are gay. They are excellent teachers and we have long since moved on from the prejudiced view that their pupils might somehow be at risk. In fact the last incident of that kind in our school involved a relationship between a respectably married male teacher in his fifties and a fifteen year old girl."

"Let your father get his coat off, "rejoined Joyce. "I'll put the kettle on and then let's talk about something else - anything else" she added with a hint of desperation.

However, despite Joyce's ruling, after some general chat the conversation drifted back to the Session meeting and Luke's worries that what had been a focussed and harmonious body of people might now become more fractured, more distrustful of one another. He was also aware that the opinions he had expressed would be discussed outside the meeting and could harm pastoral relations with some of his parishioners.

"I think it's perfectly reasonable that you should express a view." This was Joyce speaking. "It's not as if you're saying that sexual promiscuity is acceptable, or adultery, or prostitution."

"Mum's right," said Anne, "and I think you will find that a lot of people agree with you. I have no doubt that sexual orientation is something you are born with. Homosexual people are not automatically bad people any more than are heterosexual people. The trouble with demonising a person because of their sexuality is that they then feel the need to conceal it or to express it in secret and dangerous ways."

As Anne spoke Luke recalled an incident from his youth when one of his father's ministerial colleagues was arrested in a public lavatory and subsequently convicted on a charge of gross indecency. The sad tale was featured prominently in the local newspaper and there was no question but that the minister had to go. Without hesitation he resigned his charge and, with his wife and family, left the area. Looking back on that incident from half a century ago Luke wondered whether, if that man had been free as people are today in areas other than the Church to be open about his sexuality and take a same sex life partner, might he not have continued to have an effective ministry. By all accounts, as far as Luke could recall, he had been a decent man and a well-liked, conscientious parish minister.

Luke's thoughts also drifted to his school friend, Derek, who had died a distressing and untimely death some years previously from AIDS related pneumonia. Luke and Derek had first met as twelve-year olds sitting the bursary competition for a prestigious fee paying school. They were both successful and Luke still recalled the parental delight when the results were announced. He remembered too his own pride and joy at the handsome new bike which was his reward. Even with three speed gears it had cost a fraction of six years of school fees!

Both boys had shown musical promise from an early stage – Derek on the violin and Luke on the piano – and throughout their years of secondary schooling a regular feature of the annual School Concert was a duet by the boys. Encouraged by the Head of Music they would attend concerts given by the Scottish National Orchestra or the Glasgow Choral Society. Luke still had a copy of Handel's *Messiah*, a Christmas gift from a member of his father's church choir and recalled attending a performance of the oratorio with Derek, the pair of them sitting following the score. Thinking back to it he couldn't help thinking that they must have resembled a teenage Niles and Frasier. After school the boys went their different ways – Luke to University, Derek to Music College. However, they kept in touch and would meet up from time to time in the holidays and occasionally perform together at church concerts.

Towards the end of school there was some talk amongst the senior boys about Derek's sexuality. The term "gay" (good as you) was not then current so a rather more pejorative vocabulary was relied upon. Some years later the sixth form gossip seemed to be proved wrong when Derek announced his engagement to a fellow musician – an attractive young soprano – and asked Luke if he would be best man. Luke was delighted to accept, the marriage took place and in due course a child was born. Derek's career prospered and took him to London with one of the big orchestras. His wife's singing career also prospered, though her work kept her and their young daughter mainly in Scotland.

After a few years it became apparent that the marriage was in trouble. A separation was arranged and then a divorce. By now Luke was in Dundee and Derek would come to visit from time to time. On one occasion a visit coincided with the AGM of the congregation which was usually followed by some musical entertainment. Generously Derek agreed to give a short recital which had been hugely appreciated.

It was on one of these visits that Derek announced that he was gay (the term now being in vogue) and that he had a new male partner, a fellow musician. The sixth year gossips had been right after all. In truth neither Luke nor Joyce were shocked by the announcement and assured Derek that this made no difference to their friendship. He would continue to be welcome, as would his partner, in their home. Looking back Luke wasn't sure just how confident he had been about the final part of that offer. After all, their home was a Church of Scotland manse – and that was twenty years ago – but, in the event while Derek did visit from time to time he was always alone.

It was on one of these visits that Derek dropped the bombshell. He had been diagnosed HIV positive. He wasn't sure what that meant in terms of his ongoing health. He was well at the moment and having treatment but, clearly, it was a worry. Again Luke and Joyce affirmed their continuing friendship, support and welcome. Luke remembered that this was still in the early days of AIDS. He also remembered the line taken by some of his ministerial colleagues that AIDS was a 'gay plague' a judgement from the Almighty. "That will be a great comfort to Derek," he had mused.

Within a couple of years Derek had contracted full blown AIDS and died, still in his 40s and at a point where his musical career was really beginning to take off. His widowed mother telephoned to break the news and asked Luke if he would be willing to conduct the funeral. How could he have refused, even if he had wanted to? The funeral took place in the Church where Derek's family had worshipped and a young Derek had attended Sunday School and Boys' Brigade. A large congregation gathered, many having made the journey from London. Luke recalled that, with so many musicians in attendance, the singing had been inspirational. But it was the family group that particularly struck him. They arrived and left together in the funeral car, hugging and holding hands. They sat together in the front pew – Derek's widowed mother, then in her eighties, his ex-wife, their daughter (now a young woman) and Derek's partner. Everyone present wore a red HIV/AIDS awareness ribbon. It was one of the most moving funeral services Luke had conducted and, looking back, he realised that this had been a turning point in his thinking about homosexuality and the Church – a significant milestone as he travelled steadily from Paul towards Luke.

Two cases where people had been forced by social and religious convention into relationships which were not appropriate to their given sexualities and where the outcome for both, and for those whom they loved and were loved by, had been deeply tragic. Luke thought again about Mary White at the Kirk Session meeting who had asked her fellow elders (assuming they were all 'straight') how they would feel being coerced into a homosexual relationship. None had responded but her point, no doubt born of the experience of having a gay daughter, had certainly struck a chord with Luke.

"You're a hundred miles away, Dad. Have you heard anything Mum and I have been talking about?"

"I'm sorry dear, what were you saying?"

At this point the telephone rang.

"I'll get it," said Luke.

"Who was that, at this hour?" asked Anne when Luke returned.

"It was Brian MacFarlane, the Session Clerk," replied Luke. "He has been collating the views of the Session and thought I would like to know that only two of the elders had indicated an intention to leave the Church of Scotland if the Assembly gave a green light to openly gay ministers. I think I can guess who they might be. Apparently, none indicated they would leave if the Assembly refused."

6

A minister needs to be a "self starter." The typical parish minister works on his or her own and without day to day supervision. Their office is a room in the privacy of their own home but much of what they do is highly visible in terms of personal encounters and public engagements. For Church of Scotland ministers there is also a strong tradition of serving the wider parish community and not just the members of their own congregations.

The next morning Luke and Joyce lingered over breakfast. Anne had already left for her meeting.

In the early years of his ministry Luke had felt somewhat uncomfortable about not going out to work. He regularly found himself the butt of the well-worn joke about ministers working only one day a week and, certainly, it had taken a while to establish a degree of self-discipline with regard to his use of time. In college they had been told that there were two risks in having a job with little in the way of set hours. The first was that you became very lazy; the second that you worked morning, noon and night seven days a week. The important thing was to establish a pattern – mornings in the study for reading, sermon preparation, bible study, correspondence; afternoons visiting house bound parishioners and those in hospital; evenings for church meetings and visits to those not available during the day; and on top of this marriages and funerals and the conducting of two Sunday services. What was that joke about a "one day week"?

In all three of his parishes Luke had let it be known that Monday was his day off and he tried to stick to that. Inevitably, though, things would arise, like the wish of a bereaved family to have the funeral on a Monday. Luke would invariably agree, out of pastoral sensitivity towards grieving parishioners.

He was also a strong believer in parish ministry. One of his professors at Divinity College had stressed that a Church of Scotland minister was 'minister to a parish, not chaplain to a congregation'. Throughout most of his ministry there had been an assumption that the parish minister would conduct the funeral service of a deceased parishioner, whether or not a member of the Church and Luke adhered to this principle. Once, in his first parish, he had officiated at the funeral of a young Catholic woman who had taken her own life, the priest having declined to officiate. In Luke's view the congregation was not a religious social club for the benefit of its members; it was, rather, an agency of Christian witness and service within the wider community. It was therefore a matter of concern to him that some of his colleagues took a harder line and were not always willing to respond to the undertaker's call to assist a bereaved family. Their argument was that if the Church had played no part in people's lives what purpose would a Christian funeral serve? Would that not be the Church conniving in hypocrisy? Certainly it was now much easier to arrange a humanist funeral than in the early years of Luke's ministry but Luke still found it hard to turn away those who came seeking Christian consolation in time of trouble. At the same time he knew from one friend, who was minister of a large Glasgow parish, that such a commitment could mean two or three funerals of strangers in a week. Luke's answer was that assistance should be made available to the minister, perhaps through specially trained members of the congregation, so that the parish church could be seen as ministering to the spiritual needs of individuals in distress.

One of the many social changes that Luke had observed over nearly forty years of ministry was that more and more people seemed to work from home. To that extent he did not feel so different from his parishioners and, in any event, he had established an effective working pattern with, be believed, a healthy work-life balance. On this basis he had no qualms about extending breakfast this morning after the difficult Session meeting of the night before and Joyce seemed equally in no particular hurry to get her day underway.

"Do you remember that pulpit exchange in the States," she remarked, "when the sole topic of conversation seemed to be the Church's attitude to homosexuality?"

It had been back in 1991. An opportunity had come up for Luke to exchange pulpits and manses with the Rev Dr James Pierce, a presbyterian minister from Northern Virginia. Back in the 1970s Dr Pierce had undertaken post graduate studies at St Mary's College, St Andrews, gaining a PhD in New Testament studies, and was keen to show his family something of Scotland. Luke and Joyce had seen the advertisement he had placed in the Church of Scotland's magazine *Life and Work* and had responded. This would be a good chance for them too, he and Joyce had thought, and perhaps the last family holiday before Anne and Richard, then well into their teens, rebelled against holidaying with Mum and Dad.

Luke's duties that summer had consisted mainly of preaching on Sundays with most of the pastoral work being undertaken by an Associate Minister. This left time for exploring Washington DC - the Lincoln Memorial, Capitol Hill, the National Cathedral, the Air and Space Museum - and also for visits to historic sites such as George Washington's Home at Mount Vernon, Thomas Jefferson's home at Monticello and John Kennedy's grave at Arlington National Seminary.

That year the General Assembly of the Presbyterian Church in the United States (PCUSA) was meeting at Baltimore in nearby Maryland and the hot topic was a report on the question of whether self-avowed practising homosexual persons could be ordained as ministers. Two years previously the United Church of Canada had decided that they could – a decision which had lost them members, money and some congregations. Luke had gone to Baltimore to listen to the debate which had produced powerful, indeed passionate speeches on both sides of the argument. He remembered wondering how long it would be before the Church of Scotland General Assembly would have to face this question, with all its potential for fundamental disagreement amongst ministers and church members. At the same time he remembered thinking that this was precisely what being Protestant or Reformed was all about.

For Luke an extremely important part of his own Church's system of government was that it allowed liberty of opinion in points of doctrine which did not enter into the substance of the faith. The question then arose as to whether something under discussion was or was not of the substance of the faith, but that then became a matter of debate amongst the faithful, not something which was determined by some distant hierarchy and handed down on a take it or leave it basis. In the courts of the Church of Scotland ministers and elders had an equality of voice and vote. Luke recalled the first General Assembly he had attended, accompanied by an elder from his Glenburn congregation. On most issues they voted in opposite ways, leading Luke to feel somewhat aggrieved at what felt like a cancelling out of his vote. But then he realised that this was how the system worked and that his elder probably felt equally aggrieved. The Baltimore debate had been painful at points and the outcome disappointing for those seeking to allow openly gay men and women to become ministers; but Luke also remembered thinking at the time that it was good that we could have this kind of open debate in our Churches.

"Do you know, Joyce, twenty years later the whole matter still rumbles on in the States," remarked Luke. "I had a look at the PCUSA website the other day. This year their Assembly voted, by a narrow majority, in favour of changing ordination standards so that ministers will no longer require either to be married to someone of the opposite sex or to remain celibate. Apparently a proposal to the same effect was defeated last year, but people just won't let the matter rest. The website explains that this year's decision will need to be referred to all the presbyteries of the Church but already those who lost out in the debate are saying the decision was a disgrace and it will be overturned by the presbyteries."

It was back in that American summer of 1991 that Luke and Joyce became acutely aware that, while people often talked of sexuality as an 'issue', it was in fact much more than that in the way it impacted upon individual lives. As they lingered over breakfast, reminiscing over their American exchange, they recalled how they had been entertained one evening to dinner by a neighbouring minister and his wife. They too had been in Baltimore for the debate but had seen it in much more personal terms. Over dinner they had told Luke and Joyce that their son, Mark, had 'come out' at university. This had been something of a shock to his parents. It was not the life style they would have chosen for him. However, realising that this disappointment would be as nothing compared to the grief of alienating and losing their son they came to terms with the situation and continued to love and accept him for who he was. After graduating Mark moved to San Francisco to work and after a couple of years he developed a serious relationship with another young man, Cliff and they set up home together. Some months later Mark asked his parents if he could bring Cliff on his next visit home. He would like them to meet him. The parents acknowledged to Luke and Joyce that this felt awkward but they judged that they had no choice but to agree. In the event the visit went well and they were surprised at how well they took to Cliff who was a most likeable young man.

A couple of years passed and then the parents learned the shattering news that Mark, their beloved son, was HIV positive and had become quite unwell. He and Cliff remained together in their home in California but just a year before Luke and Joyce's visit Mark had died. Strangely (or so it had seemed to the parents) through their son's illness a bond of shared grief had formed between them and Cliff and, as they readily acknowledged, no wife could have cared more lovingly for a dying husband. Such, indeed was their affection for and gratitude to Cliff that, on discovering he would be on his own for the Christmas following their son's death (his own parents having disowned him) they invited him to Virginia to share Christmas with them. Luke and Joyce recalled being truly touched by such kindness and generosity. In the event Cliff declined the invitation which at least spared the grieving parents further pain. Their daughter, married with two young children, had made it very clear that if her late brother's partner came for Christmas she and her family would not.

"My goodness, look at the time," Joyce suddenly announced. "It's almost 10 o'clock. I must get on with my day. "Me too," responded Luke, heading off to the study to make a start on Sunday's sermon.

7

Preaching is a core element in a minister's job description. This is why in many churches the pulpit occupies a central position. Nowadays, the very term has a rather old fashioned ring to it and ministers regularly experiment with different approaches. Some choose to speak less formally from a lectern rather than use the "six feet above contradiction" pulpit. Others opt to split the sermon into short sections interspersed throughout the service with singing or readings in between. But, however, approached, the task is to be taken seriously, with time set aside for proper preparation. Over the period of the consultation many ministers will have wrestled with the question of how to preach on the underlying issues.

Luke was a strong believer in preaching from the lectionary. This is a three year cycle of Bible readings for each Sunday of the year. These include a passage from the Old Testament, a passage from the New Testament Epistles and a reading from one of the Gospels. Luke regarded the lectionary as a good discipline since it directed the preacher to bits of the Bible he or she might not otherwise have considered. It was then necessary to read these passages and to consult commentaries on the texts. Only after such study should the preacher begin to prepare the sermon, doing so in such a way as to relate the insights of the given Bible text with the contemporary experience of his audience. By approaching sermon preparation in this way Luke judged that his congregation would be exposed to a breadth of Bible readings over the year and that he would not fall into the trap of choosing to ride one of a limited selection of hobby horses each Sunday.

What never ceased to amaze Luke, though, was how often the set readings for any given Sunday spoke to the current moment. This appeared to be the case as he perused the passages for the following Sunday, particularly a passage from 1st Timothy which contained phrases such as "Remember Jesus Christ" and "avoid wrangling over words." The Gospel reading – and Luke, being his father's son, always had a reading from the Gospels– was from Luke chapter 17 and recounted an incident where Jesus was confronted by ten lepers – social outcasts – who cried out "Jesus, Master, have mercy on us."

Luke was well aware that by the time Sunday came round the previous evening's Session meeting would be "the talk of the steamie." Perhaps I should just grasp the nettle, he thought, and use the sermon to set out the issues before the members of the congregation. It seemed to Luke only fair that, while the General Assembly was formally consulting members of Presbyteries and Kirk Sessions, the wider membership of the Church should be kept informed on a matter which was proving so difficult for all denominations to deal with.

Here is the text of the sermon he prepared and preached (with some *ad libbing*) the following Sunday:

My friends, you will be well aware that churches around the world have been challenged to look again at Christian teaching on human sexuality, particularly with regard to homosexuality. Less than 50 years ago homosexual activity, even between consenting adults in private, was a criminal offence but over these years we have seen enormous social changes, not only with regard to homosexuality, but in attitudes to sexual conduct more generally. For example, when Joyce and I were married in the 1960s the question of our living together before we were married just never arose. Our parents would have been appalled! But today it is very common for people to live together before marriage - and not just young people. The widow and widower who meet up in later life may equally want to test the relationship and have regard to wider family sensitivities before tying the knot. Indeed, I would say that the majority of couples I now marry have already set up home together. The old phrase 'living in sin' just doesn't sit comfortably in our vocabulary today – at least not in mine. Indeed, there has always seemed to me something unhealthy about focussing on the sexual aspect of human relationships to the exclusion of all others.

The Church has also relaxed its position on divorce and re-marriage within the lifetime of many of us. Prior to 1959 Church of Scotland ministers were not permitted to officiate at a marriage service where either party was divorced and had a surviving former spouse. That rule has been relaxed and, while there is still a conscience clause for ministers, most clergy, having satisfied themselves as to circumstances and local sensitivities, will agree to solemnise such unions.

Of course, in a number of respects the sexual revolution has gone too far, with the painful consequences of increased teenage pregnancies, a massive rise in the number of abortions and the trafficking of young women for prostitution – an issue commendably taken up by the Guild. All of this the Church rightly condemns, both for the way the lives of so many people are blighted through the exploitation of the vulnerable, but also for the way sex has become a commodity, an end in itself as distinct from a precious component of loving and committed relationships.

But the big challenge we now face as a Church has to do with Christian attitudes to homosexuality and, in particular, whether the Church of Scotland should accept into its ministry individuals who are open about their homosexuality. As you know last year a minister living in a civil partnership received a call to a congregation in the full knowledge of his circumstances and the Presbytery upheld that call. Some members of the Presbytery appealed that decision to the General Assembly which dismissed the appeal and endorsed the decision to induct the minister. At the same time the Assembly appointed a Special Commission to consider all the issues, to consult widely and to bring a report to the General Assembly of 2011. Last Tuesday evening, as most of you are no doubt aware, our Kirk Session met to study the consultation material prepared by the Commission and the elders individually replied to a series of questions asked by the Commission.

What does the Bible say on the matter?

Well there are some very clear texts and those who strongly oppose the opening up of the ministry to practising homosexuals, including those in a committed civil partnership, place a strong reliance on these. For example Leviticus 18:22 states: "You shall not lie with a male as with a woman"; Genesis 19 tells of the destruction of Sodom as a judgement on the men of Sodom who demanded that Lot give over to them male guests for their sexual pleasure; in Romans 1 Paul lists female and male homosexuality amongst a catalogue of ungodliness and wickedness and in 1 Corinthians 6 he warns that, amongst others, male prostitutes and sodomites will not inherit the kingdom of God (the list also includes adulterers, the greedy, drunkards and thieves); Jude at verse 7 of his short epistle refers in admonitory terms to the destruction of Sodom and Gomorrah.

This seems straightforward enough. After all we refer to the Bible as the Word of God and, as one of the elders said the other evening, if that is the case then we can't just pick and choose which bits we like. There are many who would agree with that.

On the other hand there are those who don't think it is quite as simple as that. For example we would want to applaud Lot in Genesis 19 for refusing to give up his male guests to the besieging mob at the door of his house. But the story goes on to tell how Lot offered the lust filled gang his two virgin daughters instead. "What!" I hear you say. Yes that's in the Bible. Is anyone going to say that makes it all right? Of course not! So we are beginning to pick and choose. And the denunciation in Leviticus comes alongside a series of regulations governing the ritual slaughter of animals, the offering of sacrifices and foods which may and may not be eaten. We readily acknowledge that these strictures have no relevance to our lives as Christians today. Once again, it seems, we are picking and choosing.

And when we look at marriage itself as practised in Genesis it is not exactly a model for us to follow today. Polygamy was common and when Abraham and his wife Sarah were unable to have a child Sarah's slave girl, Hagar, became a surrogate and bore Abraham's child. The society depicted in Genesis was patriarchal and women and children were, in effect, the property of the husband or father. If a man committed adultery with another man's wife the offence was not so much infidelity to his own marriage vows as the violation of another man's property.

In a similar way some interpreters of the Bible will try to distinguish between the things Paul writes which reflect the timeless truth of the Gospel and those which reflect the cultural norms of his own day – and, dare I say, even his own personal opinion. For example nowhere does he condemn slavery, but we do because we live by different social values from the Graeco-Roman word of the first century. And when it comes to the specific issue of homosexuality we can note that his condemnation comes within a wider denunciation of a range of licentious and orgiastic sexual conduct which we would certainly join in condemning today. We can also note that, while the Bible has powerful models of same-sex friendships – David and Jonathan, Ruth and Naomi – its writers would certainly have no familiarity with our contemporary concept of committed and faithful life long relationships enshrined in what we call civil partnerships.

So where does this leave the Bible as the Word of God?

Well the first thing to say is that the Bible itself points to Christ as the Word made flesh. The words of the Bible witness to Christ but it is Christ who _is_ the Word. This is how St John unfolds the great mystery of the incarnation in the opening verses of his Gospel. This is also why, in our own Church, we refer to the Scriptures as <u>containing</u> the Word of God. Some will interpret this as meaning every word of Scripture but, as we have already seen, that raises the problem of God appearing to condone, if not actually encourage, some pretty nasty things. This is why there are those who believe that God continues to reveal new things about our world and that we cannot and should not ignore new insights into human genetics, biology and psychology. For example, the prevailing assumption with regard to homosexual behaviour is that it has been a choice – a wrong choice. But what if our sexuality is something which is a given, something we cannot change? As long ago as 1983 a General Assembly report spoke of homosexual persons "as a group that has suffered more than its share of oppression and contempt." If, as is increasingly argued, our sexuality is what we are, like race or gender, then that oppression and contempt becomes even more concerning.

The verses we read from 1st Timothy contain advice from the apostle Paul to his young disciple Timothy. He urges him to pass on the Gospel through his ministry and at verse 8 declares: "Remember Jesus Christ, raised from the dead, a descendant of David – that is my Gospel." As today we struggle in the Church with this divisive matter it is important that we remember Jesus Christ who is the Word of God and focus fully on him.

Those who support a move to ordain openly homosexual persons as ministers note that Jesus said nothing at all on the subject. Opponents counter that this means that Jesus would simply have assumed and approved the status quo. But this kind of argument, like the earlier discussion of Leviticus and Romans, leads us to something else we read in Timothy. Timothy is to remind his people of Jesus Christ, but then he is to "warn them before God that they are to avoid wrangling over words, which does no good but only ruins those who are listening."

At the end of the day that seems good advice. On the question which is before us people on different sides of the argument will produce Bible texts to justify their position and there will be no agreement other than an agreement to differ. This is why it was regarded as quite a big step forward three years ago when a group of people, drawn from both sides of the argument, collaborated to produce a General Assembly report setting out their different stances and agreeing that the proponents of both points of view sincerely believed that their opinion was in line with the Word of God revealed in Jesus Christ. This is good, for at the end of the day the Church is a diverse body of individuals seeking to understand the Bible and apply its teaching in their own lives. No one group has a right to say "we are the true Church and you are heretics." Rather we are called to live together with our differences.

We also read a passage from Luke chapter 17 about Jesus restoring ten lepers to the life of the community. Lepers were social outcasts for fear of contagion and, while leprosy doesn't impact on our society literally as it still does in some parts of the world, we are familiar with the concept of the social outcast. Indeed, as that Assembly report from which I quoted a few moments ago suggests, the Church acknowledges that homosexual people have known the stigma of the social outcast.

Now this is a risky passage to use in this context because in the story Jesus healed the lepers and there have been those and, I dare say still are, who believe that homosexuality can be cured. Last year the then Prime Minister, Gordon Brown, issued a posthumous apology to Alan Turing for his treatment in the 1950s. Turing was a brilliant mathematician and today we owe him a great debt for his early pioneering work in the development of computer science. During the war he worked at Bletchley Park and was a key figure in breaking down German naval codes. In 1945 he was awarded an OBE for this work.

Turing was homosexual and in 1952 he was arrested on a charge of indecency along with another man who had spent a night at his flat. Turing was given a choice between imprisonment and probation conditional on his agreement to undergo hormonal treatment designed to reduce libido, in effect, chemical castration via oestrogen hormone injections. He accepted this alternative. Two years later he committed suicide.

In one of the great prayers of the Church Reinhold Niebuhr asked: "God grant me the serenity to accept the things I cannot change, the courage to change the things I can and the wisdom to know the difference." Luke tells us that Jesus healed the lepers but what was important for them was that this healing meant their restoration to society. Not all healing takes the form of changing the things we can. Sometimes it involves the acceptance of things we cannot change and of people we cannot change. Apartheid came to an end in South Africa and civil rights were affirmed in the United States, not by black people becoming white, but by their being accepted for who and what they are as equal members of the human race. On this basis the Gospel story can and does speak to the matter before us. The restoring of the outcast doesn't always involve changing the one who is outcast; it involves changing the attitudes of those who judge certain individuals and groups and delare them to be outcast.

I learned recently that I shall be a commissioner to next year's General Assembly and we all await the report of the Special Commission which is likely to be published in the spring. We have seen the pain and the distress which engaging with these issues can cause, not least with regard to ordaining practising homosexual men and women and inducting them into parishes.

Please pray for the Church and for all of those who will be called upon to take significant decisions over the coming year. But, above all, please remember Jesus Christ and avoid wrangling over words.

8

The congregation is the basic unit of church life. Congregations vary considerably in size –from a couple of dozen to well over a thousand. The concept of the parish church continues in rural areas but is less meaningful in towns and cities where people are freer to choose which church to attend. The phrase "gathered congregation" is sometimes used to describe those churches which offer a particular style of worship or preaching and attract members from a wide area. As a result of declining membership many ministers find themselves ministering to two or more congregations in neighbouring communities.

The following Sunday Luke duly delivered his sermon. The church was well filled, as it was most Sundays. There was a strong tradition of church going in the community. Also, over the eight years he had been minister Luke had established a reputation for diligent pastoral care and well prepared worship. In addition he served as chaplain in the local primary school, conducting assemblies and giving occasional support to teachers in religious education. Both he and Joyce had a friendly manner and neither found it difficult to pass the time of day when they met people in the street or in the local shops. In fact, on one occasion Luke coincided with a new mum and baby in the check-out at the local supermarket and arranged a provisional date for the baptism while they waited. Luke smiled when he recalled this. His own father, in the time worn phrase, 'wouldn't have been seen dead' doing the family shopping. Similarly, the Rev Andrew would rarely venture from the manse attired in anything other than dark suit and clerical collar. Things were more relaxed now and Luke, like many of his colleagues, was content to 'dress down' when not formally on duty.

Luke also had a reputation for straightforward preaching and for illustrating his sermons with reference to current concerns. Back in college days his Practical Theology professor had advised that ministers should prepare their sermons with the Bible in one hand and the daily newspaper in the other. This came naturally to Luke because he was an avid reader of newspapers and began and ended each day with the BBC news. And on a Sunday morning he never left the manse to take the service without a final check of the BBC News website. He recalled a colleague who was mortified when he discovered that he had conducted worship on Sunday 31 August 1997 in complete ignorance of the death of Princess Diana earlier that morning and, in consequence, had made no reference to the tragedy.

Luke's congregation was also something of a broad church, as the Church of Scotland claimed to be. It served as parish church to the village of Capelaw which had expanded into a small town, with a population mix of people who lived and worked locally and others who commuted daily to nearby Edinburgh. On Sundays there were those who travelled to other congregations, mostly in Edinburgh. These included a number who in the 1950s and 60s had been in at the beginning of new housing schemes and instrumental in starting up new church extension charges. Even though they had long since moved away they felt a loyalty to these roots and a responsibility to what were now small and struggling congregations, often in areas of multiple deprivation. Then there were some who had moved out of the city more recently but travelled back to the suburban congregations where they continued to hold leadership roles. Finally, there were those who travelled to share in styles of worship which they found particularly congenial, whether the high liturgy and fine music of St Giles' Cathedral or the gathered fellowship of a conservative evangelical congregation where the focus was on strong and substantial Bible based preaching.

This Sunday exodus still left a significant number of regular church goers who liked to worship locally, to have their children attend Sunday Club and to enjoy conversation with friends and neighbours over coffee after the service. It also left a breadth of views across the liberal/conservative spectrum and throughout the week the church halls provided accommodation for a prayer meeting, Bible study group, Alcoholics Anonymous, Guides and Brownies, Playgroup, Scouts and Cubs, the Guild, a Pilates Group and several other church and community organisations. This was how Luke liked it – the Parish Church at the heart of the community.

It is not always easy for a minister to 'read' a congregation's reaction to a sermon. Luke recalled preaching in a colleague's church one Sunday and taking forgiveness as his theme. As he shook hands with the members at the church door a stern looking gentleman fixed him with a steely glare and muttered: "Jam for sinners." So much for the good news of salvation, thought Luke. Now this morning he had been heard largely in silence but the most common reaction at the door was "That was very interesting, Mr Paul – a lot to think about."

I'll take that as a positive response, thought Luke. Others just shook hands in the normal way and said little as they left the service.

However, during the course of the ensuing week Luke's mail-bag was somewhat larger than usual and not all of the feedback was positive. In truth this was the first time in nearly forty years of ministry that Luke had had any written feedback to his preaching, except on one Sunday in Dundee when BBC Radio 4's morning service had come live from his church. He remembered being particularly taken by a pleasant note and enclosed cheque from a lady in Suffolk. She thanked him for the service and explained that the Church of England had linked a number of villages under the one vicar and there was a service in her village only every second Sunday. On the Sunday when there wasn't a service she sent her offering to the Church which was on the wireless.

Here are some excerpts from the letters Luke received:

- Thank you for having the courage to tackle such a difficult and controversial subject. It had always seemed obvious to me that gay people shouldn't be ministers but now I'm not so sure.

- I found your sermon on Sunday very disturbing. If you set out to give a dispassionate account of the issues you failed miserably. It was quite clear to me where your sympathies lie. In light of this my wife and I have decided to seek another congregation where the preaching is based on the Gospel and not political correctness.

- I was so grateful for what you said on Sunday. As you know our older daughter is lesbian and now living in a civil partnership. That came as a shock at first but we now enjoy very happy family relations in a way we could not have imagined two years ago. I found your words very affirming and I am sure many others, who may not take the trouble to write, will have done so as well.

- I am sorry that the Church of Scotland is having to devote time and energy – not to mention money- to this question. What on earth is it costing to consult 40,000 elders? And what is there to consult about? The Bible makes it very clear that homosexuality is an abomination and no amount of fancy words and clever arguments can change that. Please can we have some proper Bible teaching and focus on some of the real problems of the world.

- As you know I'm in my final year of psychology at Edinburgh University and I was very interested in what you were saying on Sunday. Do you think it would be possible for me to see the report of the Special Commission when it becomes available? I have heard that they have been seeking expert biological and medical opinion on the matter.

- I know the usual thing with anonymous letters is to put them in the bin but please read this first. After one or two disastrous relationships with the opposite sex I have realised that I am gay and for the first time have met someone with whom I can envisage spending the rest of my life. I'm ashamed that I don't feel able to sign this letter but that perhaps merely underlines the difficulties people like me face, particularly in the Church. I hope we might talk soon but, meantime, thank you for your openness and acceptance.

- I come to church on Sunday to be lifted up above the problems of this world and to focus on matters spiritual. For heaven's sake – there is enough sordidness and sex on television everyday without having to endure it on Sundays as well. What is the Kirk coming to? John Knox must be birling in his grave! Please no more.

Luke replied to all of these letters, except, of course, the anonymous one, even though he had a good idea who it had come from. However, he would respect the individual's privacy and hope that in time they might find the confidence to come and talk. He was sad that one couple felt the need to look for another congregation but relieved it wasn't a larger number. In his reply to them he offered to call and discuss their concerns but recognised that the important thing was that they should find a spiritual home which met their needs and if he couldn't provide it then, no doubt, others could. He wished them well and thanked them for their support in the past.

By now it was time to start thinking about next Sunday's sermon which he resolved would address less contentious matters. And then on Monday he and Joyce were going to Fife for a few days to look after the grandchildren. Richard, their son was attending an accountancy conference in London and his wife, Alison was accompanying him. Three days with five year old Marcus and three year old Katie would certainly force him to turn his mind to other things.

9

Ministers, like politicians, can be fiercely protective of their families. Someone once famously described a manse as a "public house". We know what they meant.

Luke and Joyce had two children – Anne, whom we have met, and Richard who was two years younger than his sister.

Luke remembered a book in his father's study entitled "Sons of the Manse". He had dipped into it and gleaned its general thrust which was to extol the advantages of being brought up in a Scottish manse. Writing in the 1920s the author illustrated this thesis by pointing to a number of highly distinguished men whose fathers had been ministers of the Kirk.

The theme had been returned to in recent years with reference to Gordon Brown, David Steel, Douglas Alexander and, highly appropriately in the twenty-first century, mentioning also daughters of the manse such as Sheena McDonald and Wendy Alexander. And only the previous year Luke had read an article by Professor Tom Devine in a Sunday newspaper in which he had noted that some of the greatest figures of the Enlightenment, such as William Robertson, Adam Ferguson and Thomas Reid, were themselves ministers of the Gospel or sons of the manse, such as Francis Hutcheson.

There was, though, another side to all of this. Luke still simmered with resentment when he remembered an incident from Sunday School. He was ten years old and had been selected to recite from memory the 'motto text' – a passage from the Bible which the pupils were expected to memorise during the course of the week. For whatever reason Luke had had other priorities and it was clear from his stumbling effort that he had not done his homework. He could have taken a dressing down from the Superintendent like any other young scholar. However, what really stung was the addendum to the effect that more might have been expected of the minister's son.

The manse could be something of a goldfish bowl and, of course, it belonged to the congregation who had the responsibility of maintaining it. This was a mixed blessing. It was obviously an advantage to have a substantial family home provided and maintained. But there was a downside. Powerful elders could give the impression that they owned the manse family too. Luke recalled a colleague who had got into trouble for displaying Scottish National Party posters on the manse windows during a General Election campaign. An elder who was a Tory councillor had objected and was certainly not mollified when the minister pointed out, rather ingeniously Luke thought, that the posters were on the inside of the windows and therefore within his home as distinct from outside on church property!

Manses were often large, draughty and not maintained to the highest standards. Heating bills could be considerable and the cost of installing central heating and double glazing beyond the means of the congregation. Also, what happened if a minister died or, as could and did happen, the manse marriage ended for other reasons? The answer to that question was that the family had six months to vacate and, while some help would be forthcoming from the Church of Scotland, the loss of the family home in such circumstances could only add considerably to the pain. Retirement too meant a move, usually away from the area, so as not to get in the way of a new ministry. Some ministers managed to make provision by buying a property to rent out, usually with assistance from a working spouse. This could either become the retirement home or be sold when the time came with a view to buying something more suitable.

From time to time the Church debated the question of manses and there were those who argued that ministers should be free to make their own living arrangements like other people. The problem was that parishes varied so much. A minister's stipend would not be able to fund much in Bearsden or Cramond and in rural areas there may not be anything particularly suitable other than the existing manse which provided both living and working accommodation.

It pleased Luke and Joyce that their children had largely avoided the goldfish bowl syndrome. They were still quite young when they moved from Glenburn to St Fillan's, Dundee with the result that much of their childhood and youth had been spent in an anonymous suburban house. The church there also had an office where Luke met with people and this protected the family's privacy to some extent. At the same time, when accepting an offer by a kindly member of the congregation to look after the children to let Luke and Joyce go out for an evening, Joyce always felt pressure to ensure that the manse was clean and tidy.

Joyce also laid down another privacy protection rule to which Luke strictly adhered. Those familiar with Church of Scotland services will know that they usually include a spot where the minister speaks to the children. If truth be told many ministers find the children's address more challenging than the sermon. Perhaps this is wise because often it is the part of the service many adults like best. There is therefore the danger that the minister be tempted to use this time not so much to teach the children as to entertain the grown ups.

Joyce, herself a teacher, had two rules for children's addresses:

    (1) no cheap laughs at the expense of a child;

    (2) no stories which could possibly be linked to our own children.

Luke followed these rules meticulously – not just because he feared the lack of lunch if he didn't but, remembering his own childhood, he fully endorsed them.

By the time Luke left Dundee Anne and Richard had flown the nest. It did not seem likely that either would aspire to high political office like the other 'manse children' mentioned earlier, but Luke and Joyce felt satisfaction that the manse upbringing had given their children an exposure to Christian values and some valuable insights into human nature; for example, into how communities worked, how people related to one another and, above all, how everyone needs encouragement and support from time to time.

Anne had always been something of a free spirit. As a toddler she had loved fun and always seemed to know how to push the boundaries. As a child she was something of a tomboy and loved sports. At secondary school she was playing hockey for the 1st XI by fourth year and also represented her school in tennis tournaments. She was an avid reader and her decision to apply to study English at University seemed a natural choice. Her application was successful and she was accepted by her first choice, Edinburgh University, where she gained a decent honours degree. Her teachers considered her capable of a 'first' but she had adopted what she called 'a more rounded approach' to university life. Entering fully into the various opportunities on offer she gained a hockey blue, became involved politically through the University Labour Club and sang with the Renaissance Choir. Following University she went to Moray House to train as a teacher and from there to Argyll where she was offered an appointment as a teacher of English in a local authority comprehensive school. She proved popular with colleagues and pupils alike, once again involving herself in the extra-curricular side of the school. She joined the local branch of the Labour Party and that was how she met Archie, a solicitor in the town who would become her husband. At Anne's insistence the wedding was held in Argyll which she now considered to be home, her parents having moved from Dundee where she had grown up. She had never lived in Capelaw. Luke took part in the service along with the local minister and members of the Edinburgh University Renaissance Singers provided the music. After her marriage Anne continued to teach, taking on additional responsibilities for Guidance and, as we have already seen, becoming involved in the work of the General Teaching Council for Scotland. Archie's law practice also kept him busy. At the same time he remained hopeful of being adopted as a parliamentary candidate for a winnable Holyrood seat.

Richard was a very different child, so much so that some expressed surprise on learning that they were brother and sister. It would not be fair to say that Richard was introverted but he was certainly less extrovert than his older sister. Joyce judged that as a toddler he had observed Anne pushing the limits and, noting these limits, rarely went beyond them. His favourite toy was Lego and he would spend hours engrossed in some construction project or other. He was also very musical and took to the piano lessons his parents arranged in a way which Anne had never done. He did not particularly shine at school but put in a solid performance, particularly in maths and science. As far as sports were concerned he showed a natural aptitude for golf and came under the tutelage of a teacher who looked after the small school golf team. He was also a mad keen supporter of Dundee FC and, as a boy, regularly persuaded his dad to ensure that the sermon preparation was complete in time for them to watch the football at Dens Park on a Saturday afternoon. He was canny with his pocket money and, while his big sister was usually 'broke' Richard was generally in funds and in a position to offer her a loan on reasonable terms.

From school it seemed natural that Richard should pursue accountancy and this he did at Dundee University. He also kept up his golf, matching his sister's hockey blue with his own golf blue. After graduating he was taken on as a trainee in the Dundee office of one of the large national accountancy firms and there, a few years after qualifying as a Chartered

Accountant he became a partner. He and Alison met at University where she was studying pharmacy. They were married in Alison's home church in Fife, again with Luke assisting the parish minister, and made their home in the East Neuk. For Richard this was a reasonable commute to the office, though much of his work took him out and about in the Fife and Angus area. This meant that many days he could start from home. He also calculated that, if he was patient, he would eventually be admitted to membership of the Royal and Ancient Golf Club at nearby St Andrews. Meantime, Alison readily found a job in a local Boots, switching to part time work when the children came along.

So it was that on a Monday afternoon in late October Luke and Joyce set off across the Forth Road Bridge heading for the East Neuk. They both loved the road which followed the coast north from Leven, up through Lundin Links, Lower Largo and Elie. To their right the Firth of Forth opened up before them as they looked across to Gullane and North Berwick. Berwick Law was clearly visible and, if you knew where to look, the ruins of Tantallon Castle. Joyce smiled and said: "Do you remember the holiday at North Berwick when the children were young? It was a filthy wet day and we were looking for an indoor pursuit. You suggested Tantallon Castle so we set off thinking it might be like Crathes or Glamis. Only when we got there we discovered it was a roofless ruin."

"Happy days," rejoined Luke.

The plan was that they should arrive in time to share in the process of bathing and settling an excited pair of grandchildren into bed, something they would have to manage on their own for the next couple of nights. Then they would enjoy a civilised meal with Richard and Alison who were due to set off for London in the morning.

10

In those churches, such as the Roman Catholic Church where priestly celibacy is the rule, the rationale is that the priest is, in effect, married to Christ. Thus freed from other family responsibilities he can devote his whole life to the service of the Church. In those churches, such as the Church of Scotland, which allow clergy to marry and have a family life, the rationale is that this enables them to share and thus better understand the life experiences of many of their parishioners.

As Joyce and Luke had anticipated Katie and Marcus were watching for their arrival and came rushing out to greet them. "Gracious me, "exclaimed Alison, "give Granny and Grandpa time to get out of the car and come into the house."

"My, how they are growing," Joyce observed "and I do like Katie's grown up hair style. What happened to my little baby? And look at you Marcus. Aren't you getting a big boy. Are you going to school all day now?"

It had been a couple of months since Luke and Joyce had seen their grandchildren. There was much catching up to do, but eventually the car was unloaded, Joyce and Luke had deposited their things in the guest bedroom and everyone was gathered round the kitchen table as the children had their tea.

"Richard hopes to be home sharpish tonight," said Alison. "But you know how it is when you are to be away for a couple of days. There's always something to tie up before you leave the office. Once the children finish tea they normally watch some television or a DVD. Marcus is big on the Mister Men at the moment – especially Mr Bump. I can't believe stuff I read as a child is still on the go all these years later."

"Goodness," said Luke, "I used to read the Mister Men books to Richard when he was a boy. I'd love to see the DVDs."

His wish was granted as after tea he and Marcus settled down to watch the antics of Mr Bump. Marcus particularly liked the bit where Mr Bump was trying to prop a ladder against the wall of his house and managed to break just about every window. Then there was Mr Jelly who was terrified when a falling leaf brushed against the window of his bedroom and Mr Forgetful (I can identify, thought Luke) who rarely failed to live up to his name. Best of all for Luke was Arthur Lowe's narration in classic Captain Mainwaring style.

Meanwhile Joyce caught up with her grand-daughter whose current favourite activity was an interactive edition of *The Very Hungry Caterpillar* with stick-on stars and sun, strawberries, oranges, cup cakes - and all the other elements of Eric Carle's classic children's tale, not forgetting the beautiful butterfly which the caterpillar became. In Katie's copy the "stickies" had been on and off the pages so often it was amazing that they had any stickiness left at all.

And then it was bath time, bedtime stories and lights out.

By this time Richard had arrived home and greeted his parents – his mother with a hug, his father with a handshake. He wasn't particularly into men hugging men – even within the family circle. "It's good of you to hold the fort," he said "and if there's anything you're not sure of the children will keep you right, especially Katie. I'll just pop up and say good night to them and then I'll be back down to declare the bar open."

Over a pre-prandial glass of wine Richard caught up with his parents and also got an update on Anne and Archie's news. Joyce fretted sometimes that her son and daughter didn't seem to have much direct contact. It appeared that she and Luke were the main channel of communication between them. But she kept this thought to herself. "They're fine" she replied. "Anne stayed with us a couple of weeks ago when she had to come to Edinburgh for a Teaching Council meeting. You know what they're like. She and Archie are as busy as ever with work and politics. I don't know where the politics comes from. We're not a particularly political family but Anne certainly got fired up at University. Archie is a candidate for next year's Holyrood elections, though it's not a particularly winnable seat. But he says he's working his passage and hopes that next time round he might eventually become an MSP. Winnable or not, Anne will certainly be out knocking on doors for him next spring."

"And how's the church, dad?" This was Richard after dinner, once they were ensconced in the sitting room over coffee and a dram from Luke's first parish. "I gather you had your Session meeting to discuss the gay minister question. How did that go?"

Luke summarised the discussion of that evening. He then narrated how he had decided to preach on the matter the following Sunday and the reaction to his sermon. "One couple have left the congregation, and I'm sorry about that; but I had sensed before that perhaps I was a bit too liberal for their tastes. Things seem to be settling down again, though. There was a good turnout at church yesterday and we just need to wait now for the Special Commission's report."

"You know I'm not really with you on this one dad," said Richard. "I don't believe I'm homophobic. In fact one of our partners is gay and he and I get on very well together, despite the fact he beat me at golf last weekend. Of course the church should be open to all but I believe the ministry is a special calling and should be governed by special rules. In fact it is already. If one of my colleagues cheats on his wife and has an affair that won't cost him his job – provided it doesn't affect his work as an accountant. But it's different for a minister. It's part of a minister's job to uphold moral standards, so a minister who commits adultery rightly loses his job. His credibility would be shot through."

"But I also have a practical concern as a church treasurer," continued Richard. "Since last year's General Assembly agreed to allow that gay minister to be inducted to a parish three members of our congregation have cancelled their standing orders to the church. Including the gift aid these lost contributions total nearly £4,000 and that's a lot of money for a small country kirk. I might have persuaded them not to act so precipitately by stressing the need to support our own congregation; but when our own minister expressed her support for the pro-gay lobby there was no chance."

"But it can't be right," interjected Joyce, "that wealthy givers should dictate church policy. That feels a bit like cash for honours – or at least cash for influence. Is there not something in the Bible about giving without seeking any reward?"

"I don't think that's fair," responded Alison. "Richard hasn't told me who these individuals are but I can guess who one of them is and he's a really decent guy who is something of a local philanthropist. It just so happens that he takes a traditional view on matters of faith. I agree with him and don't accept that makes us homophobic. Richard mentioned his gay colleague. Well, we've had him and his partner for dinner and they are delightful. But I just cannot get my head round the idea of a couple like that in the manse and there are lots of people in our church who think like me."

"And the rules allow for that," Richard chimed in. "If at work we refused to appoint someone to a job on the grounds that they were gay we would be breaking the law. That would be clear discrimination. The Church applies that law in respect of its employees – for example people who work in the church offices. But parish ministers are not employees in that sense. They are holders of an office and that puts them in a different category. Our session clerk, who is a lawyer, has advised us that the Equality Act and the Employment Equality (Sexual Orientation) Regulations do allow for discrimination, provided it is in order to comply with religious doctrine or to avoid conflicting with the strong religious convictions of a significant number of a religion's followers."

"That is true, "Luke replied, "and the consultation paper which came out in the summer mentions this. But it also mentions that legal opinion is divided. It points out as well that the regulations do apply to ministers who are not parish ministers, for example those who work under contracts of employment. This would include people like hospital, university or military chaplains. There is also a school of legal opinion which thinks the UK government could be vulnerable if an individual took a case to Europe challenging these opt outs."

"But, Richard, while I'm speaking, I would also question your original comparison with adultery," Luke continued. "Of course the law doesn't allow two gay people to marry, but would you not make a distinction between a homosexual person in a civil partnership, with all the commitment that entails, including fidelity, and someone who was sexually promiscuous? If it is the case that our sexuality is given rather than chosen, and there is now a mechanism for same sex couples to make a life long commitment, could the same moral rules not apply to both marriage and civil partnership? The gay equivalent of adultery would then be infidelity to the civil partner, not simply the fact of being gay and sexually active within such a partnership."

"That all sounds somewhat contrived to me, dad," responded Richard. "Look, I'm an accountant, I conduct audits, there are rules, procedures, protocols, all written down and I follow these. The way I see it is that there are also rules, procedures and protocols for Christians and these, too are written down in the Bible. Once we start picking and choosing which bits to follow, where do we end up." (Where have I heard that before, thought Luke?) Richard continued: "I'm not convinced that sexuality is entirely given and never chosen. And I will be interested to see what expert evidence the Special Commission produces, if they can find two experts who agree! As I've already said I am not homophobic. I agree that the Church should be open to all. I just feel that the man or woman in the pulpit should either be married or celibate. That seems to me to accord with the teaching of the Bible."

"Well," said Joyce, "it's getting late and you two have an early start in the morning. We're not going to solve the Church's problems tonight but please don't let's fall out over it. Your father will be at the General Assembly next year. Rather him than me!"

11

On their ordination ministers promise to play their due part in the administration of the Church. In effect this points to church life beyond the parish. The Church of Scotland does not have bishops to manage its affairs. Rather it maintains a principle of parity of ministers and relies on ministers and members from around the country to play their part in formulating and implementing church policy at the national level.

Over his nearly forty years of ministry Luke had not been much of a man for church committees. By contrast, some of his colleagues had made a career out of this aspect of Church life. Presbyteries and the General Assembly work largely through a committee system. This covers various areas of interest – ministry, mission, overseas work, stewardship and finance, Christian education, worship, doctrine, communication – the list goes on and on. And then there are *ad hoc* groups set up, mainly at presbytery level, to deal with particular situations which arise. For example there might be a breakdown in relations between a minister and the local elders; or there might be a whiff of scandal which has to be investigated, delicately and discreetly. Luke recalled reading about a case in the late nineteenth century involving a middle aged, married minister who attracted the attention of the presbytery. It was noted by those who take an interest in such things that on more than one occasion the minister had escorted a young, unmarried lady home from the evening service. He was charged with the offence of "culpable imprudence." This was not a particular indictment that Luke had come across though he expected there was plenty of it around. In recent years (he surmised on account of his seniority) Luke found himself called upon from time to time to take on such trouble shooting roles.

For those who were into committee work in a big way the route to follow was the one which took them to Edinburgh several times a year to serve on a General Assembly committee. These bodies offer a promising career ladder and hold out the prospect of promotion to a major convenership. This involves reporting to and fielding questions from members of the General Assembly. Conveners also account for the work of their committee in the media, getting their name in the papers and perhaps even being interviewed on radio or television. Many a Moderator has come to the Kirk's highest office having served as a convener.

The other career option afforded by these General Assembly committees is akin to the civil service route. The larger committees have a permanent Secretary who has responsibility for the implementation of the General Assembly policy in his or her area and for managing the staff of the relevant department. Whereas the Convener serves a four year term and speaks on behalf of a committee the Secretary is a paid employee whose tenure of office is not fixed.

Luke had no interest in the Church's internal politics at either Presbytery or General Assembly level, but one area which did excite him was ecumenism. In his theology finals he had opted for the specialist study of Ecumenical Theology and throughout his ministry he had championed events such as the Week of Prayer for Christian Unity, sometimes, it has to be said, in face of considerable apathy from colleagues and members of his congregation. Cynics would say things like, "If we can't worship together all the time, what is the point of getting together for a shared service on a dreich January evening?" Luke's answer to this was that it was better to take small steps than to take no steps at all. After all, had Jesus not prayed that his disciples might be one? Surely we could not just ignore that plea. No less a person than Scotland's First Minister had once referred to sectarianism as 'Scotland's shame' and all right thinking people agreed. Some of the stuff which went on around Rangers and Celtic football matches was a disgrace to Scotland and an embarrassment to Christianity, both Catholic and Protestant. Luke had approved when a few years previously the Kirk's Moderator and the Cardinal Archbishop of St Andrews and Edinburgh had very publicly attended an 'old firm' Celtic v Rangers game in Glasgow together.

In the early 1990s Luke had become involved in the work of ACTS (Action of Churches Together in Scotland). This was a new ecumenical body which created a forum for dialogue and joint action involving many of Scotland's churches. The two largest members were the Church of Scotland and the Roman Catholic Church. However, this was an area where size didn't matter and smaller denominations were given an equal voice at the table. Luke remembered during his college days reading reports of World Council of Churches gatherings attended by Christians from all over the world. They had come, some vast distances, to worship, to study, to pray and to reflect on how they could offer an effective and united witness to a divided world. One particular phrase from such a gathering in Lund, Sweden stuck in Luke's mind. Known as "the Lund Principle" it holds that churches should act together in all matters except those in which deep differences of conviction compel them to act separately. Luke fervently believed this. He further believed that there was far more on which the churches agreed than disagreed.

Not surprisingly the one General Assembly committee on which Luke was happy to serve was the Ecumenical Relations Committee. His membership was during a period in the mid 1990s when a serious attempt was being made to bring together five Scottish denominations, including the Church of Scotland and the Scottish Episcopal Church. Luke had been a boy in the 1950s when the General Assembly, urged on by a negative press, had roundly rejected a report prepared jointly by representatives of these two churches, fearing that it was an attempt to foist bishops upon the Kirk. Would this new 1990s initiative suffer a similar fate? Luke had been a member of the group which had worked on this particular aspect, seeking to align elements of presbyterianism and episcopacy – no easy task. In the century following the Reformation of 1560 that had proved impossible and it was to prove no easier at the turn of the twentieth and twenty-first centuries. Luke was disappointed, but not entirely surprised when the General Assembly of 2003 instructed the Ecumenical Relations Committee to pull out of the talks.

Meanwhile, during his ministry at St Fillan's, Dundee Luke found a new outlet for his ecumenical instincts right on his doorstep. Situated within his parish was a convent, home to a closed order of Roman Catholic nuns. He had passed it often enough and given it no more than the merest of passing thoughts. But it happened that one of his elders, a painter and decorator to trade, was successful in quoting for a major redecoration of the premises and carried out the work entirely to the satisfaction of the nuns and the diocesan authorities. At the conclusion of a Kirk Session meeting the painter, Bert Scrimgeour by name, came up to Luke and asked if he might have a word. "Sure," Luke replied. "We're finished nice and early for a change. Let's have a comfortable seat in the vestry."

So it was that Bert told Luke about his assignment – how he hadn't been quite sure what to expect, never having been in a convent before – but how friendly and helpful the nuns had been. "Some things were a little strange," he confided. "The prioress said they would give us tea mid morning and mid afternoon in their refectory. When we went there everything was set out – cups, milk and sugar, even biscuits. And then, as if by magic, the teapot appeared on a turntable through a hatch in the wall for us to help ourselves. We weren't sure whether to say thank you back through the hatch!"

"Anyway," Bert continued, "I happened to mention to the prioress (by the way her name is Sister Clare) that I was an elder here and she was very interested – asking about St Fillan's and the minister and the sort of things we did. And, to cut a long story short, she wondered if you would care to call sometime to say hello. Apparently they are quite autonomous. You wouldn't have to check with the bishop or anything like that – though you might want to check with the Kirk Session," he added with a mischievous twinkle.

"Mmm," said Luke. "I suppose I am the parish minister and the convent is in the parish – even though my writ doesn't run there. Thanks for passing on the message. Leave it with me and I'll let you know what I decide."

After relaying this conversation to Joyce over a cup of tea in the manse it didn't take Luke long to decide. "Of course you must accept," was Joyce's immediate reaction. "It would ungracious and churlish not to."

"I agree," said Luke, "but I would feel a bit awkward. What does a minister say to the prioress of a closed order of nuns?"

"Well you could start with 'It's lovely to meet you and thank you for the invitation'," answered Joyce, then adding more softly, "but I know what you mean. Why don't I come with you – not that you'll need a chaperone, I'm sure."

And so it was agreed. Bert had given Luke the contact details for the prioress and times when it would be convenient to telephone. He and Joyce would visit and then he would inform the Session afterwards. That felt better and less like asking their permission.

Two weeks later Joyce and Luke called at the convent. They were shown into a pleasant but rather plain room. Across the middle of the room was a grille on the other side of which were gathered about a dozen smiling women dressed in brown habits. As Luke and Joyce approached one of the nuns introduced herself as Sister Clare and said how welcome they were. She spoke appreciatively of Bert's workmanship, of the sensitive way he and his men had worked around their regime and of how interested she had been in hearing about his church. She had also heard from Father Peter, the priest who acted as their chaplain and celebrated mass for them every day, how committed Luke was to ecumenism. She went on to say that, while she and her sister nuns were not exactly Luke's parishioners, they all shared a common vocation in Christian ministry – albeit rather differently exercised. Luke and Joyce both warmed to these sentiments and the little smile which accompanied the final comment.

Luke responded with similar warmth and gradually the conversation expanded as introductions were effected. An hour passed in no time at all and eventually Sister Clare said, regretfully, they would need to conclude because a time of prayer was due. However, she hoped Luke and Joyce would come back with members from their congregation for an ecumenical service in the convent chapel. It would need to be there, she explained, because they did not leave the convent. Luke readily agreed and then, having checked that touch was permitted, he invited Sister Clare to join hands with him through the grille and suggested they each offer a short prayer.

So the meeting concluded. Joyce and Luke were directed to a side room where, they were told, a pot of tea would come round the turn. "Please help yourselves and come back soon."

To Luke's delight – though not surprise – his report of this venture to the next Session meeting was warmly received. Over the remaining years of his ministry in Dundee shared services were indeed held between members of his church and the sisters. These usually marked festivals such as Christmas, Easter, Pentecost and Harvest, with the worship planned by Sister Clare, the chaplain Father Peter and Luke. And when the time came for Luke to leave Dundee Sister Clare asked if they might make him a gift of a preaching stole. This, if he accepted, would be made by Sister Gloria who was a skilled seamstress and would be happy to discuss designs with him. Luke was delighted with this generous offer. The design he came up with was a motif linking the Celtic cross - symbol of an early and undivided Scottish Christianity and the burning bush - emblem of the present day Church of Scotland. As Luke explained, it was a matter of high principle to him that the pre-Reformation history of Scotland was an important part of the Kirk's heritage. While he and the nuns followed different traditions they were all alike spiritual heirs of Ninian, Columba, the saintly Queen Margaret –and not forgetting Fillan, who had ministered in Fife and Perthshire in the early eighth century and to whose memory Luke's church was dedicated. In years to come Luke would wear the preaching scarf with pride as a reminder of a truly enriching ecumenical friendship.

12

Presbyterianism claims no more than that it is agreeable to the Word of God. It makes no claim to be the only proper form of church government, or even the best. On the basis of Christ's prayer in St John chapter 17 an obligation to seek unity with other churches is written into the constitution of the Church of Scotland.

In light of Luke's ecumenical credentials it was highly appropriate that he should receive a letter from the Secretary to the Ecumenical Relations Committee inviting him to represent the Church of Scotland at the General Synod of the Church of England.

It is a feature of church life that Synods and Assemblies are attended by delegates from other churches. Luke had always enjoyed the session of the General Assembly when these visitors were welcomed and one or two of them conveyed greetings. It was like a mini-United Nations, with guests from every continent - some in splendid episcopal or national dress, some who came from countries where Christianity was a minority religion and some, perhaps, who had experienced actual persecution. These delegates were permitted, indeed encouraged, to take part in debates and some did so with great effect. If the General Assembly was discussing conflict in the Middle East who better to speak than a delegate from the Middle East Council of Churches? If the crisis in Darfur was on the agenda how fortuitous to have a delegate from Sudan. This, thought Luke, was one of the best things about the Assembly. People came from parishes all over Scotland and suddenly found themselves part of something so much bigger than their congregation back home. Now they really could feel part of the world-wide Church.

Luke's assignment to the General Synod was particularly appropriate as his mother, Aileen, was English and as a child Luke was regularly taken on visits to her family in Leicester. He had the fondest memories of these visit to his maternal grandparents' home in the Western Park area of the city. His mother's brother, Richard, also lived nearby in the village of Woodhouse Eaves and Uncle Richard's son, David, was just a year older than Luke. The two cousins became the best of pals and remained in regular contact until David's untimely death from cancer while only in his mid-fifties. Luke's grandfather was a keen amateur historian and a founding member of the Richard III Society. This had been established in the 1950s to rehabilitate the reputation of the king slain in 1485 at the Battle of Bosworth Field, the penultimate battle of the Wars of the Roses. "If ever there was a case of history being written by the winners this was it." This was granddad's assessment of the Tudor propaganda machine which went into overdrive following the accession to the throne of the victor of Bosworth, Henry VII. Indeed, in granddad's view the chief propagandist was William Shakespeare. It was no coincidence, therefore, that Luke's uncle had been christened Richard, the name which Luke passed on to his own son. Bradgate Park and House, birthplace of Lady Jane Grey, queen for nine days after the death of Henry VIII, was also a favourite place to visit. Luke wondered whether this early association with lost causes might now be finding expression in his increasing sympathy for the case against a blanket ban on openly gay clergy in the Church of Scotland.

Through this affectionate association with his English relatives Luke was proud to regard himself as an Anglo Scot. As such, when it came to football or rugby internationals he would have nothing to do with the 'support any team but England' brigade. However, when England was playing Scotland his loyalty was unequivocally to the team from the north.

The General Synod was to meet in London in November of 2010 and this would be the opening session of a new five year synod. Luke was looking forward to attending and was determined to make time to prepare. Certainly there would be Synod papers to read, but it would also be helpful, he thought, to read up more generally about the Church of England and the issues it was currently addressing.

Luke was aware that there were similarities and differences between the two churches north and south of the border. Both assumed the role of national churches in looking beyond their own memberships and seeking to serve the life of their respective nations. Also both were regarded as 'mother churches' – the Church of England to the world wide Anglican Communion and the Church of Scotland to the presbyterian family of churches. A third similarity, he appreciated, was that both churches faced deep divisions over the issue of gay clergy. How, Luke was keen to observe, would this play out at the General Synod?

If these were common themes there were also substantial differences, not least in the form of church government and ways of relating to the state. Not only did the Church of England have bishops, a number of these bishops sat in the House of Lords and played their part in the affairs of Parliament. By contrast the Church of Scotland operated a presbyterian form of church government and exercised no constitutional role in parliament or government. There were also differences in the way the two churches related to their world wide networks. The Anglican Communion was a much more formal entity than the presbyterian family of churches. The latter was largely an historic and emotional attachment to Scotland by churches around the world which were begun, either by the efforts of Scottish missionaries, largely in Africa and Asia, or by Scots émigrés in countries such as Canada, Australia and New Zealand. By contrast the Archbishop of Canterbury was head of the Anglican Communion whose bishops met once every ten years at the Lambeth Conference. This meant that while, on the particular issue of gay ministers the Church of Scotland might want to take note of what other presbyterian churches were doing, the Church of England was in a position where its decisions and the decisions of other Anglican churches had much more in the way of implications for the whole world wide Communion. With regard to homosexuality such decisions were proving both highly problematic and extremely divisive.

Luke's preparatory reading reminded him of all this. In particular, on the question of gay clergy, he noted that Anglican bishops from around the world meeting in the 1998

Lambeth Conference had upheld traditional teaching that marriage is between a man and a woman and that Christians who were not married should remain celibate. However, notwithstanding that majority stance over 100 bishops had signed a letter of apology to gay and lesbian Anglicans.

Five years later came the row over the proposed consecration of Canon Jeffrey John as a suffragan bishop. Canon John was a priest who lived openly in a celibate domestic partnership with another man. This was an arrangement which the Church had acknowledged to be acceptable. As a House of Bishops pastoral statement on civil partnerships put it: "The Church should not collude with the present assumptions of society that all close relationships necessarily include sexual activity." Notwithstanding the non-sexual nature of Canon John's relationship the prospect of his becoming a bishop so alarmed many traditionalists within the Church that he eventually withdrew and was, instead, appointed Dean of St Albans Cathedral. But even then a consequence was that a number of churches within the diocese withheld financial contributions as a protest. Luke noted the irony of St Alban being the first English martyr.

That same year, 2003, in the United States of America, the diocese of New Hampshire elected Gene Robinson, an openly gay priest, as bishop and he was duly consecrated. This caused wide consternation throughout the Anglican Communion but was followed by decisions of a number of Anglican provinces around the world to permit, or at least to declare a policy of not necessarily forbidding the ordination of a non-celibate gay individual to the ministry or the blessing of same-sex unions. These provinces included Brazil, Mexico, Southern Africa and (Luke observed with particular interest) the Scottish Episcopal Church. These decisions resulted in other provinces around the world declaring a state of 'impaired communion' with some Anglicans in the United States withdrawing from the Episcopal Church USA and aligning with provinces in Africa. One can gauge something of the tensions within the Anglican Communion by considering a statement of the Anglican Church of Nigeria. This referred to the "evil of homosexuality which is a perversion of human dignity." The statement went on to encourage the National Assembly of Nigeria to declare homosexuality illegal. On the other hand, another voice from Africa, that of no less a person than Archbishop Desmond Tutu, preaching in Southwark Cathedral in 2004 declared:

> The Jesus I worship is not likely to collaborate with those who vilify and persecute an already oppressed minority. I could not keep myself quiet whilst people were being penalised for something about which they could do nothing, their sexuality. For it is so improbable that any sane, normal person would deliberately choose a lifestyle exposing him or her to so much vilification, opprobrium and physical abuse, even death. To discriminate against our sisters and brothers who are lesbian or gay on grounds of their sexual orientation for me is as totally unacceptable and unjust as apartheid ever was.

What perplexed and distressed Luke and many others was the judgmental and intemperate way in which this particular debate was so often conducted, a point not lost on Dr Rowan Williams, the Archbishop of Canterbury. In a pastoral epistle to Anglican churches he had condemned comments by some bishops which ran the risk of inciting violence against gay men and women. Luke noted down the archbishop's words for possible future quotation: "Any words that could make it easier for someone to attack or abuse a homosexual person are words of which we must repent. Do not think that repentance is always something others are called to, but acknowledge the failings we all share, sinful and struggling disciples as we are."

Then, in December 2009 the stakes had been raised further when, again within the Episcopal Church USA, an openly lesbian woman, Canon Mary Douglas Glasspool, was elected as a suffragan bishop in the Diocese of Los Angeles. Leaders from twenty Anglican provinces meeting in Singapore the following April denounced this action, declaring that it "demonstrated yet again a total disregard for the mind of the Communion." Notwithstanding this intervention Canon Glasspool's consecration went ahead the following month.

All of this background, along with a diligent reading of the papers which had been sent out from Church House, formed part of Luke's preparation to attend the General Synod. But now the date appointed had arrived. The Synod was at hand and it was time to head for Waverley Station to catch the London train.

13

The Church of England has been described as having synodical government and episcopal leadership. In addition the Sovereign is that Church's Supreme Governor and, as such, opens the General Synod. The Church of Scotland has presbyterian government but locating its human leadership is not so straightforward. Its highest office, Moderator of the General Assembly, is held for one year only and that on a first among equals basis. Its organisation is conciliar with authority located in the courts of Kirk Session, Presbytery and General Assembly rather than in individuals such as Bishops and Archbishops. The present Queen has been present at General Assemblies in 1960, 1969 and 2002 and was, indeed, the first sovereign to attend a General Assembly in person since James VI. In years when the Sovereign does not attend she is represented by a Lord High Commissioner, an office dating back to the 16th century whose original purpose was to monitor and even control proceedings on behalf of the King.

The General Synod opened with a service of Holy Communion in the magnificent setting of Westminster Abbey. The Sacrament was celebrated by the Archbishop of Canterbury and the preacher was Dame Mary Tanner, a leading Church of England theologian and a president of the World Council of Churches. Members then moved across to

Church House, headquarters of the Church of England, where the new Synod was officially inaugurated by the Queen.

Luke recalled how his first General Assembly had similarly commenced with Holy Communion in St Giles' Cathedral, after which members walked up the Lawnmarket to the Assembly Hall for the start of business. That pattern had long since been replaced. Now the Assembly opened in the Hall itself and got straight down to business. Holy Communion was celebrated by the Moderator in the Hall at the start of a normal business session later in the week. The rationale for the change had been to affirm the links between work and worship and to underscore the connections between the sacrament and the business.

Certainly for many the General Assembly communion service was a high point of the proceedings. Celebrated in the distinctively reformed manner, the bread and the wine were passed from hand to hand, each serving his or her neighbour. This pattern always put Luke in mind of the opening verse of Richard Gillard's hymn from New Zealand:

> *Brother, sister, let me serve you.*
> *Let me be as Christ to you;*
> *Pray that I may have the grace to*
> *Let you be my servant too*

Luke also liked the inclusive way those who sat in the public gallery were offered the Sacrament. He believed it was very important that the Church of Scotland maintained an open communion table. When celebrating the Sacrament in his own church he unfailingly extended the invitation to "all who love the Lord Jesus Christ and seek to be his disciples in the world." One year he was sitting next to a blind lady at the General Assembly communion service. Some amusement was created as the bread was passed along the row and her labrador guide dog raised a hopeful head. This put Luke in mind of another hymn: *All creatures of our God and King*.

This being the first gathering of a new Synod there was formal business to be dispatched. This included the appointing of the inevitable committees and the noting of some interesting statistics. For example 35% of the elected members were attending for the first time; the proportion of female clergy had risen from 21% to 28% compared with the previous Synod and there had been a similar increase in the proportion of women amongst the elected laity membership – 46% compared with 40%. While he didn't have equivalent figures for the General Assembly in his head Luke did have a memory that around 22% of Church of Scotland ministers and nearly half of elders were women. While the gender issue had largely settled down in both churches it had not entirely gone away. There were still areas of Scotland, mainly the west highlands and a few conservative congregations around the country, which refused to recognise the ministry of women. The next big test for the Church of England was the issue of women bishops. A number of clergy and congregations had been tempted by arrangements recently put in place by the Vatican to receive them into the Roman Catholic Church should women bishops become a reality.

For Luke one of the joys of ecumenical gatherings was time away from the formal business as opportunities arose for chatting informally with other delegates. A nightcap shared with a Catholic priest from Birmingham and a couple of vicars, one from Southampton and one from Yorkshire, provided a congenial forum for comparing and contrasting the three denominations. The priest suggested that while, of course there was disagreement and dissent within the Roman Catholic Church, compared to Anglicanism and the Reformed Churches it was a much more disciplined and homogeneous body. Many Catholics around the world would be sympathetic to opening the priesthood and even the episcopacy to women but the nature of that Church would never encourage the kind of debate on the subject which had taken place in other churches. The same considerations would apply to the question of homosexuality in general and with regard to the ministry in particular. In the Anglican and Reformed traditions such issues would be subject to debate, and eventual resolution, by a process of voting in Synods or Assemblies. With the Roman Catholic Church the matter would be decided by the hierarchy and ultimately by infallible papal decree. Many faithful Catholics might be left unhappy with the outcome but would have little option but to accept the decision or leave the Church, a step not lightly taken.

In this connection Luke shared the story of a couple in his congregation who were in church every Sunday and who gave a lot of time to voluntary work for the church and also in the wider community. The wife was a member of the Church of Scotland, but not the husband. In conversation one day the reason for this came out. The husband had been brought up Catholic but, while doing his national service, had rejected much of that Church's teaching and dogma. However, out of a sense of filial duty to his mother, who was still alive, he had felt unable to take the further step of formally joining another church. He was grateful for the Kirk's broad parish, as distinct from narrow congregational focus, and for the fact that in the parish church he could worship and receive communion with his wife.

Luke went on to wonder aloud whether the Church of England, as part of the Anglican Communion, stood somewhere between the Roman Catholic Church and the Reformed churches such as the Church of Scotland. The Roman Catholic Church had a clear authority structure and decision making process. Likewise, the Church of Scotland, while taking note of what other reformed churches decide on contentious issues, would make up its own mind. However, the Church of England was one of thirty-eight provinces in the world wide Anglican Communion which, at present appeared to be being torn apart over the issue of gay clergy. The Archbishop of Canterbury, though head of the Communion could not rule it by decree. At the same time the connections amongst the provinces were more formal than those, say between the Church of Scotland and other presbyterian churches around the world. So it mattered more to the Church of England what other Anglican churches thought.

The two vicars agreed with this analysis and went on to explain that this thinking had led the Anglican Communion, following the consecration of Gene Robinson as Bishop of New Hampshire, to draw up a Covenant to which all Anglican provinces would subscribe. The intention was that this Covenant would affirm the autonomy of each province, but also commit the provinces to be sensitive to the feelings of other provinces. If it appeared that a decision about to be taken by one part of the Communion would be deeply upsetting to other areas, thought would be given to whether so much harm would be done to the whole Communion by proceeding that the better course would be to hold back. The text of this Covenant had been worked on over the previous five years and the latest draft, which had been approved earlier in the year by the Church of England bishops, was now coming before the Synod. "As the mills of God grind slowly," the Yorkshire vicar said, a resigned smile lighting up her face, "this is not for final adoption but for transmission, with or without the Synod's approval, to the various dioceses for their consideration."

While interested in following the various Synod debates Luke was particularly looking forward to the Presidential Address to be given by Dr Rowan Williams, the Archbishop of Canterbury. Luke had always been an admirer of Dr Williams who seemed to him to combine gifts of intellect and spirituality to a quite remarkable degree. The leadership team of Dr Williams and John Sentamu, Archbishop of York, struck Luke as both formidable and imaginative. In his view it must surely inspire confidence in the Church of England's capacity for renewal. If ever wise leadership was needed, surmised Luke, it was at a time like this.

Luke was not disappointed by the Presidential Address. In it Dr Williams made reference to the Covenant, describing it as a tool with which disagreement could be managed, even if it could not be resolved. With characteristic subtlety he observed that to accept the Covenant was not to tie the Church's hands but to recognise that it had the option of tying its hands if it judged, after consultation, that the divisive effect of some step would be just too costly. Referring specifically to the issue of same-sex unions he criticised the 'tribal' approach to the question, where each side of the argument believed that absolute right was on its side. Some, he suggested, regard this as almost the sole test of biblical fidelity or doctrinal orthodoxy; others believe that the Church must be brought inexorably into line with what modern culture can make sense of. Putting his authority and leadership on the line, Archbishop Rowan urged support for the Covenant. To fail to do so, he argued, was to risk the piece by piece dissolution of the Anglican Communion and the creation of new structures in which the Church of England and the See of Canterbury were unlikely to figure significantly.

Dr Williams also declared his own belief that women bishops would be a good and timely development for the Church and indicated his readiness to argue the case theologically. He also expressed his sorrow that some had already decided that they could not in conscience continue this discussion within the Church of England.

After debate the Synod agreed the Covenant but not before a powerful speech from one of the bishops. He warned that often there was a connection between good intentions and unintended consequences; and he didn't mince his words. Responding to assurances that the Covenant would not be tyrannical he accepted that that may well be the case. However, he went on to assert that the treatment of lesbian and gay Christians by some within the Anglican Communion had verged on the tyrannical and if the Covenant were to give such tyrants comfort he would be bound to resist it. To him, he declared, it felt like sending sincere and faithful Anglicans to stand in the corner until they have seen the error of their ways and can return to the ranks of the pure and spotless.

"Powerful stuff," muttered Luke *sotto voce.*

On the train back to Edinburgh Luke pondered what he had heard over the previous few days. So often, he thought, it comes down to the price that is to be set upon the unity of the Church. Certainly that is always to be sought and cherished. Both the Church of Scotland and the Church of England already included people with divergent views on subjects such as abortion, stem cell research, cohabitation before marriage, the ordination of women, to name a few issues. On this basis, Luke wondered, whether it might still be possible to hold the church together on the question of ministry and same sex relationships. This would involve finding ways to affirm those homosexual persons who felt called to ministry while protecting the consciences of those who found such a prospect unbiblical and deeply disturbing. No easy task, thought Luke – but surely worth exploring.

14

There is something of a postcode lottery in the Church of Scotland over whether a minister who blessed a civil partnership would be subject to church discipline. This is because any such action would be for the relevant presbytery to initiate. In the Church of England the local vicar's 'line manager' is an individual, namely, the bishop. In the Church of Scotland the equivalent role is the presbytery, a body made of up of fellow ministers and elders from the surrounding district.

As usual, when Luke arrived home after a few days away there was a bundle of mail awaiting his attention. He had a system for working through this. Obvious junk mail was put aside for re-cycling. Then routine stuff, such as papers for the next presbytery meeting, was kept to be opened in the study the following morning. More interesting looking items such as hand addressed white envelopes, particularly if marked *Private and Confidential*, tended to be opened immediately.

In Luke's bundle there was indeed an item which ticked all these boxes and so was the first to be opened. It was a hand written letter from a young woman in his congregation. Her name was Ailsa Macleod, a popular classroom assistant in the local primary school and a much valued helper with the church youth group. She apologised for writing to Luke anonymously a few weeks ago after his sermon on

Christianity and homosexuality (Luke's hunch as to the author of that letter had been correct) but she had needed a little time to think. She had now found the confidence to get in touch openly to ask if they might meet. As she had said in her earlier letter she had met someone with whom she could envisage spending the rest of her life. She and Liz had made the decision to enter a civil partnership and it would mean a great deal to both of them if Luke would offer a service of blessing. She would understand if he declined, because she knew that this was a difficult issue for the Church of Scotland, particularly at the present time. The last thing she wanted was to get Luke into trouble with the church authorities. She had written, rather than phoning so as not to put him on the spot and wasn't expecting an immediate response. But would he think about it and get back in touch with her in the next little while?

Like many parish ministers Luke had wondered when he would receive the first request of this nature. A number of ministers had already blessed civil partnerships and, before the existence of this legal option, same-sex relationships. Invariably these occasions had been attended by a *frisson* of controversy, but usually this died down pretty quickly and life went on as before. There were considerable sensitivities to be weighed. From the Session meeting he knew that at least two of his elders would be very unhappy if he went ahead and could make trouble for him. On the other hand he might have expected more grief after the sermon of a few weeks ago. And then there was the question of his pastoral responsibilities to Ailsa who was clearly feeling somewhat fragile. He felt quite affirmed by her confidence in him and did not want to let her down. But before getting back to her he would have a word with the Presbytery Clerk.

The office of presbytery clerk is an important one in the Church of Scotland. The presbytery is the body which oversees the work of the Church in a given area and the clerk is its administrator and executive officer. Presbytery clerks have a sound knowledge of the workings of the Church and can be people of considerable influence and authority. Unlike an English bishop they cannot instruct their clergy but they can offer advice in such a way that a minister knows it would be unwise not to follow it.

The clerk of Luke's presbytery was a retired minister, the Rev James Morrison, who had been much involved in the Church's committee work at General Assembly level. He had been clerk for around 15 years, initially combining it with his parish duties, but for the last five years it had been a retirement interest and one particularly appreciated by Mrs Morrison.

James Morrison had the air of someone who had seen it all. By those who knew him he was reckoned to be completely unflappable; to the stranger he could come across as detached and laid back. The old Scots word 'canny' summed him up to a tee. But he ran a tight ship. Presbytery meetings were well prepared and efficiently run, procedural questions confidently answered ("always sound confident," he had once advised a fellow clerk, "even when you're not sure") and points of order deftly handled. He also had a reputation for discretion, a vital quality in a clerk and was not afraid to risk a minister's displeasure by asking for a word if a whisper that all was not well in a particular parish reached his ears.

"Good to hear from you," was the friendly greeting when Luke phoned to ask if he could call round for a chat.

"Of course you can. How about tomorrow morning at 11?"

"Ideal," said Luke. "I have a school assembly at 9.30. I'll come on after that."

"Excellent," responded James. "I'll have the coffee on."

Luke had already decided that he would bless Ailsa and Liz's civil partnership. He wasn't going to ask the Presbytery Clerk if he should. Still less was he going to ask permission. Strictly speaking he didn't need permission. In matters of pastoral judgement a minister is master or mistress in their own parish and answerable only to the presbytery, not the clerk. His purpose in talking the matter over with James was twofold. Firstly, it was courteous to alert him in case he received complaints. Secondly, it would be useful to have his take on how things might play out. Luke thought this might be a first for their Presbytery.

Luke had assessed the situation accurately. James liked people to come to him saying, "Here is the issue I want to discuss. This is what I propose to do. Can we talk through scenarios and consequences?" James much preferred this approach to the alternative of "Here is the issue I want to discuss. What should I do?"

"Ministers should take responsibility for their decisions," he had once opined, "not position themselves so they can blame the presbytery clerk if things go pear shaped!"

Over coffee Luke outlined his reason for being there. He briefed James on the Kirk Session's recent discussion and the sermon he had preached the following Sunday. "Good for you," was the clerkly response. "I'd have done the same if I'd still been in the parish. But now you're dealing with the follow up, from aggrieved members who are leaving to happy members who are feeling affirmed. What was it Abraham Lincoln said about 'all of the people all of the time'. It sounds like you're doing something right."

"Well, that's reassuring" responded Luke. "Thanks for the vote of confidence. But it's strange isn't it. Here we are, a couple of old timers with eighty years of ministry between us and we're struggling to see what all the fuss is about. But some of our young colleagues, in the ministry for about ten minutes and they are so certain that they know God's mind on everything and are often quite strident with it. Joyce and I watched an episode of *Lewis* the other evening. You know, he was Morse's side kick and after John Thaw died they kept the series going with Kevin Whateley. Well the story was about a young student who committed suicide. It turned out he was gay and had come under pressure from a no doubt well-intentioned Christian group to seek a cure. And these 'Christians' were awful. In fact Joyce remarked on what kind of message is this giving about the Church? No wonder the young are turning their back on us."

"Anyway," continued Luke, "we're not here to discuss the whole issue – just what might happen once it becomes known that I'm going to bless this civil partnership."

"I think you're being a bit hard on some of our younger colleagues," chided James. "Even we were young once and very clear in our opinions. In my view the key to resolving this whole tension is learning how to disagree without being disagreeable. That's not easy when some question your very Christianity if you disagree with them, particularly on this issue. You and I believe in a tolerant and inclusive Church but how do we tolerate intolerance? At the end of the day this mustn't become a fight to the death with losers and winners. There needs to be an accommodation. At the very least I should have thought that homosexual ministers should be subject to equivalent expectations as heterosexual ones. This would mean that sexual relations be confined to a legal civil partnership in the same way as for the heterosexual minister they should be confined to marriage. It would, in my view, be completely unacceptable for gay ministers to have a license to be promiscuous as it would for those who are straight. If that were made clear it might make some who are opposed more content."

"But, to get back to the matter in hand," continued James, "Are you going to bless this civil partnership in the church? For those who are wholly unsympathetic that would be the 'red rag' option – desecration and all that. Offering a blessing at a hotel reception might not appear so 'in your face'."

"I really don't know what they want," answered Luke. I've still to let Ailsa know my decision and meet with her and her partner. I thought I'd come here first. But, if they want a ceremony in the Church it might be hard to refuse. Ailsa is a loyal and active member and does excellent work with the young people. However, my instinct tells me they will want the blessing at the reception. Ailsa is a very sensitive person. She will know that some people would be upset about the church being used for something of which they strongly disapprove and she will not want to give offence unnecessarily."

"But tell me, James," continued Luke, "what could I be getting into here? Will this be a first in the Presbytery and what exactly is the position of the Church as a whole? I think I understand it but it would be good to hear it from you."

James advised that this would be the first blessing of a civil partnership by a minister in their presbytery and also confirmed that there was no law of the Church forbidding it. "You know the position, Luke," he amplified. "The conservatives will argue that the Church's disapproval of same sex-relationships has not been changed by any new decision and so remains the default position. Indeed when the opportunity was there to make explicit provision to bless such partnerships it was not taken. On this basis they will say for a minister to conduct a service of blessing would be a disciplinary matter. Against this the liberals will argue that the Church could have gone beyond rejecting a piece of permissive legislation and actually passed a banning order. But it didn't take that step. Indeed as long as 20 years ago the General Assembly rejected a motion to this effect. There have been one or two cases in recent years when ministers have blessed civil partnerships and there have been threats of discipline, but they have never come to anything. I can think of one or two of our colleagues here who will be upset when they find out and might make a fuss; but I don't think you need be too concerned."

"Now, tell me about the General Synod," continued James. "How was it?"

Over a second cup of coffee Luke gave a brief account of his attendance at the Synod in London and then it was time to go. "Thanks for your time, James and your good counsel as ever. I'll keep you posted."

15

Ailsa is typical of many young people who have been sent to Sunday School by parents anxious to give their child a grounding in Christian faith. However, by teenage years the pattern has fizzled out and there is no progression to committed adult membership of the Church. Faced with this many congregations in Scotland and elsewhere are developing innovative approaches to reaching out to young people and the communities in which they are set.

That evening Luke phoned Ailsa at home to say that he was open to offering a blessing on her and Liz's civil partnership and inviting them to come and see him to discuss details. Naturally, Ailsa was delighted. She would check with Liz but was sure they could both come round to the manse one evening the following week.

Ailsa had rented a small flat in Capelaw when she came to work in the local school. In her late twenties, with an easy, friendly manner she was good at her job and well liked by her work colleagues. She had grown up in Edinburgh, where her parents still lived and, after leaving school had worked in the office of a large motor dealership in the city; but her main interest was amateur dramatics. Her school maintained a tradition of putting on a show at the end of the summer term and, to great acclaim, Ailsa had played leading roles in two productions– *Kiss me Kate* in fifth year and in her sixth year

Guys and Dolls. It would be wrong to read too much into her feisty rendition of *I Hate Men* - she had always had friends of both sexes - but it certainly brought the house down. Her *Take Back Your Mink* was also memorable. Following these successes she was enthusiastically welcomed into an Edinburgh music theatre group. This provided an important counter balance to a day job she found less than challenging.

After a couple of years of this routine Alisa decided to take a year out. Her plan was to travel round the world and to this end she had put some money by. If this ran out she reckoned she could get bar or waitress work to replenish her reserves. Since leaving school she had continued to live at home with her parents and two younger brothers, so living expenses to date had been minimal. Not surprisingly, her parents, whose sole experience of overseas travel was to holiday in Spain, were somewhat anxious about their 20 year old daughter her setting off into the unknown. It was therefore agreed that Ailsa's first port of call would be Sydney, where her father's sister had settled some twenty years previously. Aunt Jessie and Uncle Jack would be pleased to have their niece stay for as long as she liked. They had no family of their own and had plenty of space in their home in Sydney's western suburbs out towards the Blue Mountains.

In the event the planned round the world trip ended up as three years largely living and working in Australia. Uncle Jack and Aunt Jessie had done some job market research prior to Ailsa's arrival and within a few days of touching down at Sydney Airport she was interviewed successfully for a temporary post in theatre administration. Talk about landing on your feet! Ailsa soon made friends and after a couple of months moved into a rented flat, sharing with a young man from Norway and two young women, one from New Zealand, the other from Hong Kong. This proved to be an amiable and congenial ménage as all four spread their youthful wings before settling down to the serious business of life.

The New Zealand girl, Kimber (or Kimberly, to give her her full name), was a church goer and worshipped regularly in a Uniting Church in Australia congregation near where they lived. Ailsa had attended Sunday School as a child but, as her parents had sent her and her brothers to church rather than bring them, the pattern of church going never really established itself. As a consequence, by the time she reached her teens Ailsa had drifted away. She had nothing against the Church – indeed thought it did a lot of good – but she wasn't sure how to find her way back in, even if she had wanted to.

Kimber shared Ailsa's interest in amateur dramatics and the Church she attended had a youth outreach programme which included Christian theatre. The congregation was located in a rather run down, but culturally diverse area of the city and was served by an energetic minister who had a real vision for how a church could adapt and thrive in a new context. St Ronan's had started life as a presbyterian church, founded by late nineteenth century émigré Scots. St Ronan had been one of St Columba's monks on Iona and, according to legend, had driven the devil out of the Leithen Valley and blessed a natural spring in the area. To this day this is known as St Ronan's Wells and is a popular tourist attraction at Innerleithen in the Scottish Borders. However, by the early 1990s the ecclesiastical well was beginning to run dry as St Ronan's Church reached a point where its continuing viability was being seriously questioned. A diminishing number of loyal members, many travelling in from more affluent suburbs, kept things ticking over but apart from Sunday services there was little activity. In any event the inherited pattern of Scots presbyterian worship had no real relevance to those who lived in the surrounding streets. And so, when the previous minister retired closure seemed the obvious option. However, a group of members managed to persuade the congregational leadership and the Uniting Church authorities that to close shop now would be to turn their backs on a lively and diverse community and, in effect, to confirm that the church was little more than a social club for those who liked things done the way they had "aye been" (as the Scots would put it).

This was around ten years before Ailsa arrived in Sydney. In the end permission was given for the congregation to call a new minister with the promise of additional funding from central church funds for an initial period of five years. One prize asset possessed by the congregation was its building which had been well built and reasonably maintained. It was also well placed in the centre of the community, near to shops and the local train station. To cut a long story short, by the time the five year review came round the buildings were being used seven days a week for a variety of community groups, including work with aboriginals; a number of external funding sources were being tapped into and Sunday services were held every week in English and Mandarin.

The youth theatre project had begun two years before Ailsa's arrival and had two successes under its belt, *Jerusalem Joy* by Roger Jones and *A Man Dies* by Ernest Marvin. These had been staged in a local theatre as part of the church's Easter celebration and had played to enthusiastic audiences comprising largely families and friends of the performers. The next project was to be a performance of *Joseph and his Amazing Technicolour Dreamcoat* and it was with a view to this that Kimber sought Ailsa's involvement. Without hesitating Ailsa said she would be delighted. This sounded like a whole new approach to church and to teaching young people the stories of the Bible. She would be pleased to help in any way she could. One thing led to another and before long Ailsa was attending Sunday services with Kimber and becoming more and more involved in the life of this remarkable congregation. A year later she made public profession of her faith and was received into full membership of the Uniting Church.

This was an idyllic time but Ailsa knew it could not last forever. She would soon have to decide whether to make her life in Australia or return home. Her original plan had been to travel and she had done some of that. Kimber had invited her to New Zealand for her first Christmas 'down under' and after the family celebration in the lovely art deco city of Napier they had hired a car and taken two weeks to drive around the North and South Islands. Ailsa even managed a bungee jump, something which came out long after the event when her mother observed a tee-shirt with the logo "Congratulations – you did it!" "Did what?" Mum had enquired.

Her parents had finally taken the opportunity of their daughter's time in Australia to make their first visit there. "We've been here for twenty years and you've never come to see us; but better late than never," was the blunt Aussie welcome from Jessie and Jack. Ailsa enjoyed showing her mum and dad round her now familiar haunts, but they also travelled beyond Sydney – to the Gold Coast and the Great Barrier Reef, to Uluru and Alice Springs, to Canberra and Melbourne. And, when the time came to head back to Scotland, which is what she eventually decided to do, Ailsa travelled at a leisurely pace. She eased her way gently across the vast continent on the Indian-Pacific railway, breaking her journey for a few days in Adelaide then continuing west across the vast Nullarbor Plain to Perth. First she headed south for a few weeks finding a waitressing job in one of the Margaret River wineries. From there, her finances in somewhat better shape, she worked her way north, feeding dolphins at Monkey Mia, swimming with whale sharks at Exmouth, riding a camel along Cable Beach at Broome, exploring the marvels of Kakadu from her crocodile shaped hotel and eventually bidding a fond farewell to Oz on a Singapore Airlines flight out of Darwin. From Singapore she travelled north through the Malayan Peninsula and on into Thailand, finally arriving back in the UK on a British Airways jumbo from Bangkok. It was dark, it was cold, it was very early in the morning and more than three hours until her connecting flight to Edinburgh – but, as she would tell people afterwards, it was good to be home.

But it had also been a good three years and she had been very fortunate. The temporary theatre admin post had become permanent and that had given her some financial security. She had made good friends and found her work with the church, particularly the youth theatre project, quite transforming. She had also – and this was major – accepted that she was gay. Both in Scotland and Australia she had had boyfriends. Most of these relationships had fizzled out after a few dates but one had felt as if it might be going somewhere. This was during her first year in Sydney. Through work she met Rick, a stage designer from Queensland and it was evident to friends that they enjoyed each other's company. However, once things started to become more physical Ailsa knew that this wasn't for her and ended the relationship. This was painful for them both but she was honest with Rick and he accepted the situation. For the remainder of her time she enjoyed friendships with both men and women, seeking nothing deeper but knowing what her needs were and content to wait until someone with the potential to be a life partner appeared in her life.

Back in Edinburgh, aged 23, Ailsa wondered about applying for teacher training but wasn't sure if that was what she wanted. Yet she did want to work with young people. It was her mother's suggestion that she look into the possibility of training as a classroom assistant, a suggestion which she followed up and which led eventually to her appointment at Capelaw Primary School in Luke's parish. After a year travelling by bus from her parent's home in Edinburgh she decided to move into a flat in the village (which, despite its recent growth it was still called). Maggie Russell, local florist and church elder, had an apartment above her shop in the

High Street for rent and this was perfect for Ailsa's needs. She reckoned it was time she had her own place and was also keen to become involved in the life of the community. Encouraged by Maggie she began attending the local church. It was somewhat more douce than St Ronan's in Sydney, but it had a good feel about it. She volunteered to help with the youth group and soon became a valued member of the group's leadership team. From time to time, under her direction, a group of teenagers would enliven the Sunday service, perhaps with a short play acting out a Bible story, perhaps by introducing some new music to the congregational repertoire. There was general agreement within the parish that "that Ailsa" was a great asset. Would this change when news of her civil partnership became public?

16

Some young people, like Ailsa, are led into the Church through creative outreach programmes; others, like Liz, remain sceptical and turned off by their perception that the Church is instinctively against progress.

Liz was pleasantly surprised when Ailsa told her that the minister had phoned to say he was happy to offer a blessing on their civil partnership and inviting them to meet to discuss the details. She had a rather jaundiced view of the church and ministers and felt that they were not in touch with the lives of ordinary people. She didn't like the way some Christians seemed to be against people having a good time and how they always seemed to be against new discoveries in science and medicine, even though these had the potential to cure terrible diseases. Liz's mother suffered from multiple sclerosis and a cure for that would surely be a great blessing. How, then, could some church people be so sure that God did not approve of things like stem cell research? And then, equally close to home, there was the Church's homophobia, as Liz saw it. What right did ministers and priests have to condemn her life-style as sinful? "Some of them could talk!" she would observe. "What was that Jesus said about the one without sin casting the first stone?"

Despite these sentiments Liz was content to go along with Ailsa's idea of a blessing because she knew that it was important for her. But, in truth, there was more to it than that. Despite her negative take on religion and church she recognised that she and Ailsa were taking an important step and that some hallowing of their commitment would be appropriate. Also, she was prepared to be pleasantly surprised by this minister of whom Ailsa spoke so warmly. She also wondered whether he might give her a copy of the sermon he had preached on sexuality which seemed to have caused such a stir. She must remember to ask.

Liz and Ailsa had first met in the motor dealership where Ailsa had worked. Liz, who was a few years older, was on the sales side of the business – somewhat unusual for a woman - but she was good at her job and had an excellent sales record. She did weary, though, of the common reaction when people asked her what she did and, on being told, would quip; "Would you buy a used car from this woman?"

In those early days Liz and Ailsa would meet at work and sometimes socially on staff nights out and that was as far as it went. Then Ailsa left for Australia and never really thought of Liz again.

Meanwhile Liz, sensing that she had reached a glass ceiling in the motor sales business began to think of a career change. When she left school there had been some talk of her going into nursing, but she wasn't sure if that was for her. Inevitably, with her mother's illness she had some hands on caring experience, but she was looking for something more glamorous and selling cars seemed to offer that opportunity. But, as her mother's MS progressed and she saw the vital work done by the nurses who came regularly to the house, she decided the time had come to change tack. She already had the necessary qualifications for admission to nursing studies and was successful in her application to begin training. By the time she and Ailsa met up again a few years later she was a staff nurse in the Intensive Care Unit at Edinburgh Royal Infirmary.

Their meeting was at a party held to mark the thirtieth birthday of a mutual friend from the motor dealership days. Quite a few of the old crowd were there as well as a lot of people Ailsa didn't know. She and Liz got chatting and found they had so much to say to each other that they agreed to meet for a drink the following weekend. That had been two years ago. Their friendship blossomed and with that came a dawning realisation that what they had was more than friendship. It was rather a bond of love which sought nothing less than a commitment to a sharing of the rest of their lives. Acknowledging the paradox they both found this bond to be truly liberating, albeit the prospect of sharing the news with their families was daunting. Ending parental dreams of a daughter's wedding and grandchildren is something not to be undertaken lightly. In the event, things went better than they had feared. Liz's mum's cruel illness had given both her parents a perspective against which to measure new developments. Their daughter was well, their daughter was clearly happy and they liked Ailsa very much– what could be wrong with that? By contrast, Ailsa's parents were uncertain, particularly her dad, whose initial response had been to say he wanted nothing to do with it and wouldn't be attending any ceremony. But they gradually became used to the idea. Liz's appearance on the scene combined with Ailsa not having met a 'Mr Right' in Australia had sown a seed, particularly in her mother's mind, and if their beloved daughter was happy so were they.

These stories in outline were shared with Luke when the three of them met in Capelaw Manse one snowy evening a week before Christmas. "Tell me something about yourselves and what has led you to this point?" he had asked after the initial introductions. So they did. "These are great stories" he observed "and clearly you are approaching your civil partnership in a mature and considered way. As you know these are challenging issues for the Church and this is the first time I have been asked to bless a civil partnership. But I know how hurtful the comments of some church people must be to you so I am pleased that you have felt able to approach me as you have done. Now tell me what you have in mind for the blessing."

Ailsa responded: "The legal ceremony will take place in the Registrar's office in Edinburgh and then there will be a meal in a hotel for our families and close friends. The hotel has a small chapel and we would like to have a short, simple service there before the meal. Having everything together seemed a more convenient arrangement and I was also worried if we had something in the Church some people might get really upset – as opposed to just upset," she added with a smile. "We have a provisional booking for a date at the beginning of April but can change that if it doesn't suit you."

Luke smiled too and consulted his diary.

"The date's fine," he said. "Have you any thoughts yet on material for the service? You know the Church doesn't have a standard order of service for this."

"We had assumed that," Ailsa replied. "We have some thoughts but would welcome your own input, if that's OK."

"Absolutely," said Luke, "but tell me your ideas."

Liz took up the offer. "Ailsa is much more of a church goer than I ever was," she said, "but I do have some favourite Bible readings. What about that bit: Where you go, I shall go; where you lodge, I shall lodge?"

"Ah, Ruth and Naomi," said Luke; "daughter-in-law and mother-in-law and a beautiful friendship. You know it's not just about commitment; it's also a plea for tolerance. The book of Ruth was written long after the events it describes and at a time when Jews were not allowed to marry outside their faith. But Ruth is a Gentile woman who marries a Jewish man and one of their great grandchildren was to be none other than David, Israel's greatest king. So it's more than a nice story; it's a story which makes a powerful point about inclusion and exclusion."

"What about promises?" Luke continued. "Do you want to make promises to each other?"

"Yes," replied Ailsa "and we assumed that we could work on that. Can we send you something to look at and you can let us know what you think. We also thought a couple of friends might read from the Bible or a poem, or both. We have some ideas. Then there is another friend who writes his own songs and has offered to sing for us. Would that be all right?"

"Fine," said Luke. "What about hymns?"

"I had wondered about *For the beauty of the earth*," answered Ailsa. "It's one of my favourites and it talks about the joy of human love. I also like that hymn from New

Zealand which we often sing in church– *Brother, sister let me serve you*. I loved New Zealand and the hymn reminds us that we all need to be givers and receivers in a relationship. Our singer friend plays the guitar so he could give a lead. Do you have any suggestions, Mr Paul?"

"I'll think about it," said Luke. "There's a fine hymn by Brian Wren called *This is a day of new beginnings*. You might like to look at that; but it sounds as if you've already given a lot of thought to the service and that's good. It's important that you take ownership of it. I can offer some prayers and pronounce a blessing and, if you like, lead the proceedings. Why don't I draft an Order of Service incorporating these elements? You can then fill in the detail and perhaps we can meet again in a few weeks to finalise things."

"Meanwhile," he continued, "where will you be making your home? We'd be sorry to lose you from Capelaw, Ailsa."

"We're still working on that," Ailsa replied, "but we shall probably settle in Edinburgh. We're looking to buy and as neither of us has anything to sell it's a good time, with prices low and sellers, especially those who have already bought, desperate to sell. In fact we've put in an offer for a flat in Dalkeith Road. That would be on the right side of town for both of us to get to work. But we'll keep you posted."

"Can I just check something else?" Luke asked. "Do people here know about your plans, Ailsa? Have you told colleagues at school or your landlady, Maggie? I won't be saying anything to anyone but it would be helpful for me to know lest anyone mentions it to me. You know what this place is like for gossip!"

"That's a good point," said Ailsa. "I plan to say something to Maggie once we know our offer for the flat has been accepted and I expect after that word will get round pretty quickly! I'll also let my head teacher know as I wouldn't want her to learn from someone else. Actually I hope that both of them will come to the reception as they have been very kind during my time here. How about I let you know once I have told them. That way you can be prepared if there is any reaction. Can I also mention that you have agreed to bless our partnership?"

"Of course you can" replied Luke "and it would be helpful if you let me know once you start telling people. Good luck with the flat and I'll hear from you in due course."

Well, I think that's as much as we can do this evening. Let's fix a date towards the end of January to meet again and firm up the arrangements."

"We really appreciate your help and support with this," said Liz. "It's good to feel so affirmed. I only hope it's not going to cause you any grief. We know you're taking a stand here and that there is bound to be some criticism. So thank you and, if it's not an awful cheek, may I ask you something?"

"Ask away" said Luke, wondering what was coming.

"Ailsa told me about that sermon you preached in October. Would it be possible for me to have a copy? I am sure I would find it very helpful?"

"Happy to oblige," replied Luke. "I don't always stick to the script but I like to have one in the pulpit that I've prepared earlier. I'll print off copies for both if you if you give me a minute."

17

It is an important point of principle that ministers are answerable to the Presbytery to which they belong and not to the Kirk Session of their congregation. Congregations choose their own ministers and, provided the one chosen is properly qualified, the Presbytery inducts the minister to the charge. If, however, the congregation becomes dissatisfied with their minister they do not have powers of dismissal. A complaint would need to be referred to the Presbytery which would investigate. In certain situations the Presbytery could remove the minister who would then have rights of appeal. The fact that a minister cannot be dismissed by the congregation itself is an important protection against pressure and bullying by powerful individuals.

The Paul family had an understanding that they did not spend Christmas Day together. Luke was busy with services on Christmas Eve and Christmas Day. He often thought that if he had £1 for every time someone said "This will be your busy time of year" he would be a wealthy man indeed.

But it was genuinely a busy time. Over and above the normal Sunday worship there was a carol service to mark the switching on of the town Christmas lights; there were carols and a Christmas message in the old folks' home; there was the school end of term service in the Church. Then there were various Christmas functions ranging from the children's

Sunday Club parties to the Rotary Christmas Lunch. It all made for a crowded December diary.

Christmas also brought particular pastoral demands. Luke always made a point of visiting families who had been bereaved during the year, along with those who were seriously ill, the elderly and the housebound. As a result, by the time he pronounced the benediction at the end of the Christmas Day Communion service he was more than ready to put his feet up. Much as he loved his grandchildren, this was not the time to be playing hide and seek or building Lego models with them. In any event, Richard and Alison preferred Christmas in their own home, where the children could play freely with their new toys. Anne and Archie had their own child free routine with friends and were more than happy to spend Christmas Day at home in Argyll.

But the family did come together for a day between Christmas and New Year, taking it in turns to host the gathering. This year it was the turn of Luke and Joyce and the date eventually negotiated and agreed was 28th December. The arrangement was that every one should arrive mid to late morning and spend the day, catching up on family news, sharing a seasonal lunch, playing with the children, perhaps going for a walk if the weather permitted. Richard and Alison would head home to Fife early evening to put the children to bed; Anne and Archie would stay the night and set off back to Argyll in the morning. Joyce, recalling their last visit to Richard and family, made it very clear that this was family time and there was to be no discussion of "controversial issues." She didn't want Anne and Richard getting into a 'ding dong' and, anyway, it was not a subject to discuss in front of the children.

And so the family Christmas gathering passed as these things do. There were hugs and embraces, festive fare was shared, adults snoozed and Marcus and Katie brought new toys to show. These included the "humbrella" decorated with Disney characters which was Katie's pride and joy and which she insisted on keeping up during lunch. Marcus had also had a good haul of presents though, when the children were out of earshot, Alison told how she had managed to head off his proposed letter to Santa. This suggested that Santa come back at a less busy time of year when they could have a proper chat and Marcus could have a good look at his sleigh.

"That went well." This was Joyce the following morning after they had said their farewells to Archie and Anne and were straightening out the house again. "It's good to have everyone together. I do wish Anne and Richard kept in touch a bit more throughout the year, but I suppose they are both busy with their different interests."

"I wouldn't worry about it," said Luke. "We're lucky to have them both still in Scotland and living useful and fulfilling lives. And they're both very good about keeping in touch with us. Do you remember how we used to phone our parents every Sunday evening? Well, they seem to have picked up that pattern. So let's get on with the clearing up and then I need to start thinking about Sunday. It's the first Sunday of 2011. I think I'll do something on the King James Bible to mark its 400th anniversary. Perhaps I should also make the point that it's the 410th anniversary of the 1601 General Assembly which met at Burntisland, with King James present and agreed that there should be a new translation of the Bible."

"You do that, dear," replied Joyce, with a mild air of condescension. "I'll get on with the clearing up!"

At that point the phone rang. "I'll get it," said Luke.

"Hello, Mr Paul. It's Ailsa here; I hope I'm not interrupting anything."

"Not at, all. Good to hear from you and Happy Christmas to you and Liz."

"The same to you and to Mrs Paul. I didn't want to disturb you over Christmas but our offer for the flat in Dalkeith Road was accepted on Christmas Eve with entry on 1st March. I told Maggie this morning that I'll be moving out and also told her why. Frankly, Liz and I don't see why it should be some kind of secret. It's not that we've anything to be ashamed of. So our news is out there, including that fact that you have agreed to bless our partnership."

"Thanks for letting me know, Ailsa. I'm fine with that. I have a funeral at Mortonhall Crematorium this afternoon which I imagine Maggie will be attending, so I'll be prepared. Anyway, all the best to you and Liz for a good New Year and I'll see you soon."

Maggie was indeed at the funeral. The deceased had been a stalwart of the local flower club and a much valued customer. After the service she hung back as the mourners dispersed and took her opportunity to have a word with Luke as he walked to the car park.

"You'll have heard Ailsa's news" she observed, archly.

"I think I heard it before you," replied Luke in kind.

"Well, I'm pleased for her," continued Maggie. "She's a lovely lass and I'll miss her from the flat. Never any trouble, rent paid on time, place kept spotless. I'd wondered why there was no sign of boy friends but now I know why. Well, it's a free country, I say, and we're the way God made us. And good for you, Luke, giving them your blessing. Not everyone on the Kirk Session will agree with me there, but you can count on my support."

"Well, thank you, Maggie. After what you had to say at the Session I had assumed you wouldn't give me a hard time. Ailsa will have told you that she and Liz have bought a flat on Dalkeith Road. Let's hope she continues to come to the Church, though that may depend on how some people behave."

Luke's cautious instincts were not misplaced. That evening Peter Henderson phoned. He was the elder who had wanted Luke to rule at the Session meeting that there was nothing to discuss as the Bible was perfectly clear that homosexuality was wrong.

"Sorry to trouble you, Luke," he began. "I hope you've had a nice Christmas."

"Well, I did until now," said Luke to himself then, aloud, "You too, Peter. Now what can I do for you on this snowy evening?"

"Well," continued Peter, a touch awkwardly, "I was speaking to Jimmy Souter [his golfing partner and fellow elder] this afternoon and we wondered if we could maybe look in and see you sometime tomorrow."

"Sure," said Luke. "I'm free all morning. Come at 10.30 and I'll have the coffee on. Can I ask what it's about?" he added innocently.

"Can we keep that till the morning?" replied Peter." It would be better talking man to man and face to face."

Sounds ominous, thought Luke but what he said was "Suit yourself. I'll see you tomorrow."

"Well, that didn't take long," he remarked to Joyce when he put the phone down. "I think I'm about to be carpeted. Can you be carpeted in your own study?"

"Frankly, I'd show them the door and tell them to mind their own business," was Joyce's immediate reaction.

"Tempting," replied Luke but, as the good book says, 'a soft answer turns away wrath'. They're not going to change my mind but I don't want to exacerbate things by treating them too harshly. Let's wait and see what they have to say."

The next morning Peter and Jimmy arrived on schedule. Pleasantries were exchanged, coffee was poured, shortbread passed round and then it was down to business.

"Thanks for seeing us at such short notice." This was Peter's opening courtesy. "But Jimmy's wife was in Maggie Russell's flower shop yesterday morning and heard that Ailsa Macleod is a lesbian and is going into one of those new civil partnership things with another woman. What's more she heard that you're going to be there on the day and give them your blessing."

"That's perfectly correct," said Luke. "She and her partner Liz have been to see me and it's all arranged. I sense you have a problem with this. Do you want to tell me why?"

"Well I have two problems with it," interjected Jimmy. "One – I don't think a lesbian should be helping run the Church youth group and Two – I don't think a minister should be blessing homosexual activity."

"I agree," Peter chimed in. "And anyway, don't you need permission to do something like this. At least shouldn't you discuss it with the Kirk Session? I thought there was a moratorium on this kind of thing while the General Assembly was making up its mind."

"Wrong on all three counts, Peter," riposted Luke.

"One – I don't need permission to minister to members of my congregation and I would remind you that Ailsa is a very loyal and hard working member of our church.

"Two – It is not appropriate for a minister to discuss pastorally sensitive issues with the Kirk Session. Would you want your personal affairs to be discussed in that way?

"Three – The General Assembly decreed a moratorium on public statements on the issue of gay ministers and on the ordination of any more gay ministers until the whole matter had been fully considered by the 2011 General Assembly. There is no moratorium on ministering to gay church members of which there are many. I would also remind you that the minister is not answerable to the Session but to the Presbytery."

"Well," said Jimmy, trying another tack, – "has this blessing of a civil partnership ever been done before?"

"Indeed it has," said Luke "and it's usually been controversial. The first time it came to notice was nearly twenty years ago, before there were legal civil partnerships. A minister had simply agreed to a request from two women who lived together that she bless their relationship. The ceremony took place in a gathering of their families and friends and that was that. If I remember correctly, when somebody challenged the minister she asked why it was all right for the Church to bless nuclear submarines but not loving relationships between two people of the same sex."

"Anyway," Luke continued," at the next General Assembly somebody moved that ministers should be instructed not to provide such blessings. However, the Assembly refused to do so leaving it to the pastoral judgement of ministers."

"I'm sorry you feel the way you do but I hope that we can agree to differ and remain friends."

"As for Ailsa being a suitable person to help with the Youth Club I have to tell you that she has my full support and if you try to raise this with the Session I shall indicate that very clearly."

"But let me add I appreciate the fact that you have come to speak to me about this face to face rather than grumbling behind my back. While I don't agree with you I do respect you for that."

"Well, that's our style, Luke." We didn't expect to change your mind but I'm sure we're not the only ones who will be unhappy. At least, if we've heard right, you're not using the Church for the occasion."

"Well, that was Ailsa's choice, not my decision," replied Luke. "She was sensitive to people's feelings and it was also a lot simpler to have everything at the hotel. But if she had wanted the Church she could have had it and, I would remind you, that lies within my prerogative as minister. But," concluded Luke, "I do recognise the matter is contentious – and your visit here confirms that. That is why I intend to make a brief statement at the next Session meeting and to respond to any reasonable questions from elders."

With that the meeting concluded in a spirit of robust amiability and mutual appreciations of frankness and candour.

After his visitors left Luke made a note to brief his Session Clerk, Brian Campbell, on these developments when he returned from a Christmas visit to family in Ireland.

18

Elders and church members who have a complaint against their minister may refer the matter to the Presbytery. A minister who has a complaint against a colleague may do the same and it is then for the Presbytery to take a view on whether the complaint has substance and, if so, to investigate.

This rather bruising exchange with two of his senior elders concluded the year 2010 – at least as far as Luke's church work was concerned. The actual final event of the year was an altogether more sublime occasion. For several years he and Joyce had made a point of attending the Hogmanay Candlelit concert in St Giles' Cathedral and this was again firmly in the diary. As usual the event was a sell out with an audience drawn from around the world. Once again Edinburgh appeared to be the destination of choice for bringing in the New Year and the concert given by the Cathedral Choir and the St Giles' Camerata Orchestra did not disappoint. How good it was, thought Luke, to end the year in this ancient and holy place where people had worshipped over the centuries; how good to lose oneself in the beautiful and sacred music of Bach cantatas and Mozart's *Coronation Mass*. The old man knew what he was talking about when he said ministry isn't just about singing hymns and saying prayers. But, my goodness, we need the hymns and prayers of the Church and the way they bring you back to the heart of things. Suddenly the controversies of the day seem quite relative – passing clouds in an eternal firmament.

But it would be some time before the controversy which was currently troubling the Kirk would pass. Indeed, with the coming of 2011 it was only going to become more intense. The Assembly would meet in May when it would be 'make your mind up time'. And now Luke himself was becoming personally caught up in the slipstream and having some anxious moments. Not that he had any regrets about his decision to bless Ailsa and Liz's civil partnership – but he was not a controversialist by nature and he did not like confrontation. He would not let himself be bullied and he was pleased with the way he had stood up to Peter and Jimmy, but the encounter had left him shaken. He now reckoned that it was highly likely that someone would complain to the presbytery and, while reassured by his chat with the presbytery clerk, the fact remained that he had never been at the centre of a church row. Was it now possible that he might find himself the subject of a disciplinary investigation? Wow!, he thought. What a way to retire! Anne at least will be proud of her dad.

As ever, Luke's instincts were sound. Ten days into the year James Morrison, the Presbytery Clerk, called at the manse to let him know he had received a couple of letters from members of Presbytery expressing concern at reports that Luke had agreed to bless a civil partnership.

"I sense that these are quite independent letters," James added. "As far as I know these two individuals don't really know each other. I've replied suggesting that they complain to you direct rather than taking it up formally. One of them is even asking if it would be in order to move at the next meeting that the Presbytery instruct you not to give the blessing."

"And would it?" inquired Luke, with an interest that was more than academic.

"I don't believe it would," replied James reassuringly, "and I've said that to the complainer. You can't have presbyteries instructing ministers in the specifics of pastoral care. Where would it end? If someone heard that a minister was planning to marry a divorcee against whom a member of Presbytery had some objection, would we entertain a motion to instruct the minister not to solemnise the wedding? I think not. If a minister declined to baptise a baby because the parents had no interest in the Church, but a family friend was a member of Presbytery, would we allow the friend to move that the minister be instructed to baptise the child? Again, I think not."

"So," interjected Luke, "what you are saying is that you will advise the Moderator to rule out of order any discussion of the matter."

"Yes, that is what I'm saying and that is what I have told my correspondents."

"So I'm off the hook?" asked Luke, tentatively.

"Well – Yes and No," replied James.

"How very clerkly of you," observed Luke. "Go on."

"Well it seems to me that the point at which you become vulnerable is once you have done the blessing. That would be the time for an allegation to be made that you had committed a disciplinary offence. If I received such a complaint I would need to refer it to a small committee to investigate. They would meet with the complainer and with you and then decide whether there was a case to answer. If they decided there wasn't that would be an end of it. If they decided there was they could ask the Presbytery to instruct you not to do it again; or, if they thought the matter sufficiently serious, they could refer it up the line to a disciplinary tribunal in Edinburgh."

"Gulp" said Luke. "Should I be consulting my solicitor?"

"I wouldn't rush to make an appointment," smiled James reassuringly. "By doing what you are doing you are not breaking any rules of the Church. Those who are unhappy will argue that you are acting contrary to biblical teaching; but the Church has already accepted that people interpret the Bible in different ways. And, while the presbyteries refused to confirm an Assembly decision specifically authorising ministers to bless civil partnerships, it has not expressly forbidden it. Indeed on two occasions the Assembly has declined to approve such a banning order. So my advice would be just to sit tight. You may hear from one or both of those who have complained and I hope you do because it is always better to talk with those with whom we disagree, even if we end up agreeing to differ. I'm sorry about this Luke, but I thought I should make you aware."

"I appreciate that, James, but I'm getting a bit long in the tooth for this and, frankly, could do without the grief. However, I am quite clear in my own mind that what I am doing is entirely consistent with the calling of a Christian minister. I'll await contact from those I have evidently upset but won't hold my breath."

Joyce was understandably cross when Luke relayed the reason for James' visit.

"You don't deserve this. You work tirelessly for the Church and your parishioners. If I had five minutes with these people who haven't the guts to get in touch with you direct but go behind your back to the presbytery clerk I'd soon sort them out."

"That probably wouldn't help the situation," smiled Luke, "but I appreciate the thought. Perhaps we'd better not mention any of this to the children. Like you, Anne will want to come riding to the rescue; Richard will just see it as confirmation that his dad is losing the plot."

"Agreed," said Joyce, adding quickly, "agreed we won't tell the children. When did you ever lose the plot?"

Luke never did hear from those who had written to the Presbytery Clerk, but when he met with Brian, his Session Clerk, to brief him on the whole matter he told him about James's visit and the complaints he had received. He also, on Brian's advice, included reference to the complaints in the statement he subsequently made to the Kirk Session. The effect of this, as he suspected Brian had anticipated, was outrage. As Bob McEwan, the retired joiner and property convener put it: "Moderator, I don't agree with what you are doing here, but I recognise your right to make your own pastoral judgements and the lassie involved has been a great gift to our church; but you're a decent man and a good minister and if that Presbytery wants to try and discipline you, they'll have me to reckon with."

This was greeted with a general stamping of feet, the traditional way of signifying presbyterian approval.

Particularly affirming from Luke's point of view was that Peter Henderson and Jimmy Souter both made a point of nodding their heads to associate themselves publicly with Bob's remarks.

A couple of days later Luke received a phone call from James, the Presbytery Clerk.

"Good morning, Luke; James here. Just to let you know that the Business Committee met yesterday morning to prepare for next week's Presbytery meeting. They fully agree with my view of the matter we discussed a couple of weeks ago."

There's a surprise, thought Luke.

"To cut a long story short, I've been back in touch with the complainers and explained that the Moderator will rule any attempt to raise the matter out of order. They've accepted that and are content that their concerns have at least been noted by the Business Committee. I've also made them aware of how they could pursue the matter after you've done the blessing, but both seem prepared just to let the matter drop."

"That's a relief," said Luke. "Thanks again for your support and for keeping me informed. I shall come to presbytery next Tuesday with an easier mind."

And that was, indeed, the last word. Nothing was said at the presbytery meeting and none of Luke's elders raised the issue of Ailsa's involvement with the Youth Club – not publicly at any rate. There were no 'shock horror' headlines such as "Minister to bless Civil Partnership." Perhaps such stories were 'old hat' Luke thought. The world had moved on and the media had more pressing issues to cover.

And when the day of the civil partnership arrived a warm April sun shone on Ailsa and Liz as, surrounded by their families and friends, Luke led them in a service of blessing. The hymns, readings, music they had chosen fitted together perfectly; Luke's prayers were judged to have been 'just right' for the occasion. For everyone present it was in fact a first and the sky didn't fall down.

Behind the scenes, though, Luke had become aware of some tensions within the families. At a wedding the father of the bride traditionally toasts the bride and groom. What would be done on this occasion? Luke learned that a get-together of both sets of parents with Liz and Ailsa to plan the day had been quite tense at times. In the end it had been agreed that before the meal Ailsa's father would welcome the guests with Liz's father proposing a toast following the meal. Symmetry would be observed by Ailsa replying to the toast and Liz then thanking people for their gifts and good wishes. This worked well and the only real negative moment came as the party was breaking up. Suddenly Luke found himself accosted by an uncle of Ailsa's who had clearly enjoyed the excellent wine which had been served with dinner.

Jabbing aggressively at Luke's chest he began: "I'm really quite shocked that a minister – a supposed man of God – should do what you have done today. It's not right. Our society may be going to the dogs but the Church should be speaking out against it, not conniving in it. Two women pretending to get married. It's disgusting! No wonder the church is losing members at such a rate. "

Luke had experienced the drunk uncle syndrome at weddings. Usually the conversation was along the lines of why the uncle didn't go to church, but this was a whole new experience. How should he respond? Just as he was thinking that anything he said would only make matters worse the uncle's wife appeared on the scene, looking rather embarrassed.

"Come on Bill," she ordered; "it's time we were heading home. I've got the car keys here." Then, to Luke, "I suspect my husband has been giving you a hard time. I share his unease about all of this, though I would probably express it differently. But I'm very fond of my niece and, in a way, I admire your courage in doing what you've done today. I don't think our own minister would have done the same."

"Thank you for saying that," Luke replied. "We're very fond of Ailsa too and she has done great work for our church and community in Capelaw. We are living through changing times and the fact is that different ministers view things in different ways. It's always been one of the strengths of the Kirk that ministers have a degree of freedom to act in accordance with their conscience."

At that point Ailsa, who had clearly observed the encounter, appeared and said, diplomatically: "Oh Uncle Bill, Aunt Jane, I see you've introduced yourselves to Mr Paul. That's nice, but we've already taken up a lot of the minister's time today and we need to let him get on his way."

For Luke the abrasive encounter with Uncle Bill was a salutary reminder of the strength of feeling around this issue. It probably could have been anticipated that guests would have mixed views but this certainly wasn't going to detract from the day. From Luke's point of view there was really only one downside to the occasion, namely that Ailsa had been successful in applying for a new job in Edinburgh and had decided also to become involved in a church near to where she and Liz were living. She hoped Liz might eventually get involved too, but wasn't pushing it. As they said their farewells in the hotel lobby she told Luke that she was so grateful, not only for his support and friendship but for the way so many people in Capelaw had looked out for her over the years. She would miss the school, the children, the church and the whole community; but, as she put it: "In the words of that lovely Brian Wren hymn you suggested for our Blessing;

> *This is a day of new beginnings,*
> *time to remember and move on."*

It's a beautiful hymn both she and Liz had thought – perfect for the occasion.

> *Christ is alive, and goes before us*
> *to show and dare what love can do.*
> *This is a day of new beginnings –*
> *our God is making all things new.*

19

The General Assembly meets for a week in May of each year. Much of the business consists of considering reports from a variety of councils and committees and taking decisions based on their recommendations. These reports are published in what is commonly, if not always affectionately, known as the "Blue Book."

A few days after the blessing of Liz and Ailsa's civil partnership a loud thud in the manse porch announced the arrival of a heavy package in the mail. This took the form of a substantial jiffy bag, postmarked Edinburgh and bearing the imprint of the Church of Scotland offices at 121 George Street. Here was the long awaited volume of reports for the forthcoming General Assembly. Now at last Luke and others due to attend the Assembly could make a start to their homework and, in particular, discover whether the Special Commission on Same Sex Relationships and the Ministry had managed to produce a report on which everyone could agree. Luke thought that unlikely, but the eternal optimist in him still clung limpet-like to that hope.

This particular report had been kept well under wraps, though at the beginning of March a national newspaper confidently announced that nearly one in five elders would leave the Church if gay ministers were allowed. A more positive way of putting that, thought Luke, was that four out of five would not. However, the messages were mixed since, alongside this, it was reported that 20% of respondents to the consultation considered that gay people should be assessed for leadership roles in the same way as heterosexual persons. That meant 80% thought they should not, which was pretty clear. Finally, the newspaper article suggested that there might not in fact be a clear cut recommendation to the Assembly. Instead it would be suggested that a new Theological Commission be set up to prepare a further report for the 2013 General Assembly.

"Oh dear," Luke groaned to Joyce as he read this piece in the newspaper – "not another presbyterian fudge!"

"Don't be so cynical, dear," had been Joyce's reply. "Look at the last sentence of the article. It says: 'The Church of Scotland declined to comment.' That means the article is based on a selective reading of a leaked copy of the report. I would reserve judgement until you get your official copy in a few weeks time."

Luke knew that this was wise advice. He was not particularly surprised by the negative findings in relation to gay ministers but he was frustrated at the thought of yet another two years of tension and divisive debate within the Church – and he was sure that he would not be alone in this.

But now, at long last, here was the report itself. Thankfully he had no appointments that morning and could settle down in his study with a cup of coffee and see what it actually said.

It was certainly a thorough piece of work. Its various sections reported on what was probably the widest consultation ever undertaken within the Church of Scotland.

Some 25,000 ministers and elders had taken part with the matter having been on the agenda of 86% of kirk sessions and all 44 presbyteries. Other churches had also been consulted and the ways in which they were addressing the question of gay clergy were duly recorded. There was reference to scientific studies, with two specially commissioned papers from specialists in the fields of genetics and molecular biology. These reviewed the current state of scientific understanding of the causes of sexual orientation. Then there were personal stories from homosexual ministers and other homosexual Christians and their families. Luke observed that these stories had been shared with the Commission under a guarantee of confidentiality and found that both telling and worrying. At a time when the gay rights movement had won a significant measure of equality of treatment within the secular workplace it appeared that within the Church there was still a nervousness about 'coming out'. Finally, the report narrated the debate within the Special Commission itself which was, as might have been anticipated, inconclusive and ended with an inability to agree on a clear recommendation to the Church.

As the earlier newspaper leak had indicated it was suggested that further thinking on theological issues was needed. It was proposed, therefore, that a panel of theologians be set up to undertake this work and report in 2013. However, this was not entirely the 'cop out' that Luke had feared. The Assembly was at least being asked to choose between two 'trajectories' or directions of travel for this new Theological Commission.

The first of these 'steers' effectively envisaged closing down the debate by agreeing to an indefinite moratorium on the acceptance of gay ministers. The question would then be how this would affect those homosexual clergy who were already in the service of the Church.

The second option was to consider lifting the moratorium and then going on to address questions such as whether ministers in civil partnerships, who had made life long commitments in a Church ceremony, might be acceptable. Other issues to be addressed were the preparation of a liturgy for such ceremonies and arrangements for protecting the consciences of those fundamentally opposed to the admission of sexually active homosexual ministers under any circumstances.

As well as being asked to choose between these options the Assembly would also be asked to agree that ministers in same sex relationships who were already in the service of the Church should be free to move from one parish to another in the same way as other ministers.

"Less of fudge than I had feared," was Luke's verdict as he outlined all of this to Joyce over lunch. "It feels a bit tentative but at least it will allow the General Assembly to take decisions as to which road to travel."

He then went on to explain, as Joyce listened patiently, that he found three things particularly illuminating. These were the analysis of the returns to the previous autumn's consultation, the scientific papers on genetic and biological factors in determining sexuality and the personal stories of those who had met in confidence with members of the Commission.

The figures quoted in March's newspaper leak were correct, confirming that the writer of the article had indeed seen a copy of the report. But it was other and more nuanced returns which intrigued Luke. The most significant of these, he thought, was a variance in attitudes to vaguely defined 'same sex relationships' and actual civil partnerships. Out of 44 presbyteries only 7 appeared open to the prospect of a minister in a same sex relationship, with 37 opposed. When the question was asked about ministers in civil partnerships the balance shifted to 24 presbyteries open to the possibility with 20 against - a small but potentially significant majority.

Did this suggest, Luke wondered, that the issue was more about fidelity and the setting of boundaries for appropriate sexual conduct? He sincerely hoped that the Church had not reached the stage where congregational nominating committees questioned applicants on their sexual behaviour; but he readily accepted that a congregation was entitled to make certain assumptions in this regard. These would include an expectation that, if the minister was single he or she would be celibate and, if sexually active then such activity would be expressed within marriage. What the report now seemed to be indicating was that civil partnerships might be regarded as an equivalent of marriage in providing a gay minister with an acceptable context in which to express his or her sexuality.

Luke recalled the discussion (or was it more of an argument?) on this very point with his son, Richard, some months back when he and Joyce had gone to baby-sit Marcus and Katie in Fife. Would Richard be more open to this possibility now, given the responses to the consultation?

Another finding which attracted Luke's attention was that over 80% of respondents were of the view that a person's sexuality was a 'given', not a 'disorder'. There was a predictable range of views as to how homosexual persons expressed their sexuality but there appeared to be wide agreement that the orientation itself was not a matter of personal choice. From a Christian point of view, could this be put another way, Luke wondered, namely, that it's the way God made us?

This connected with the scientific evidence which, while not conclusive, Luke found compelling. Ethical restraints meant that the kind of biological research carried out on animals in the womb could not be carried out on human embryos. Evidence from human studies was therefore fragmentary. Nevertheless, the scientists were sufficiently confident to assert the likelihood of a strong biological component in human sexual orientation. The evidence, they acknowledged, did not provide absolute proof, but it was nevertheless consistent with that presumption. At the same time it was accepted that, while genes and biology have a role in determining who we are, including our sexuality, social and environmental factors also affect the choices and decisions we make as ethical beings.

All very cautious and yet, thought Luke, recalling those powerful words of Archbishop Desmond Tutu in his Southwark Cathedral sermon, why would anyone choose to be homosexual, given the degree of prejudice and worse to which gay people have been and continue to be subjected? Was this not further evidence that human sexuality was surely not a matter of choice?

Certainly, the summary of personal stories in the report confirmed the archbishop's view. Some spoke of the anguish of teenage discovery that they were 'different' from their peers. Some spoke of the pain and guilt arising from marriages which, looking back, were doomed to fail. Some spoke of growing up within the Church and trying to reconcile traditional Christian teaching on sexuality with an assurance that God still loved them. These stories Luke found particularly moving and thought again of his late friend Derek, of his father's 'disgraced' colleague from fifty years ago and of the minister and his wife who had offered them hospitality in Virginia, whose son had died of AIDS. Try as they might Luke and Joyce couldn't now recall their names. But they could remember their pain and how hard that had been for them, not least because of the added risk of alienating a daughter who could not accept that her brother was gay. How had that all resolved itself they wondered?

But things had moved on – hadn't they? There was a time when Ailsa and Liz would have struggled to find the acceptance that he and people like Maggie Russell had so recently extended on behalf of the Church. And, had the consultation carried out last autumn been carried out twenty years ago Luke was sure the results would have been very different. There had been movement and perhaps, he thought, one of the most significant factors had been that Kirk ministers and elders were discovering that some of their own children were gay and coming to terms with that – Mary White, for example, one of his elders who had spoken up in the kirk session discussion. For people like Mary homosexuality presented itself not as an 'issue' for dispassionate discussion but as a person about whom you cared passionately.

So, all in all Luke was reassured by what he had read in the report. The members of the Special Commission had done a thorough job and done it well. They had not reached agreement, but, if anything, that merely confirmed that they were truly representative of the Church. However, they had prepared the ground well and were now giving the General Assembly a choice between closing the whole debate down or moving towards the possible acceptance of openly gay individuals into the ministry.

20

Typically a minister will attend the General Assembly once every four years. Elders may attend only once in a lifetime since next time it is a Kirk Session's turn to be represented a different elder will probably be given the opportunity. It is generally acknowledged that the standard of debate is high, characterised by well informed contributions and courtesy in expressing disagreement. This last point is particularly evident when feelings are running high.

The General Assembly of 2011 opened on Saturday 21st May in the Kirk's fine Assembly Hall on the Mound. The imposing site overlooking Edinburgh's Princes Street had once been occupied by the palace of Mary of Guise, mother of Mary Queen of Scots, though there had been no Princes Street or New Town to look down on then. In the sixteenth century the low lying ground to the north of the old town, site of the modern Princes Street Gardens, was a lake known as the Nor' Loch. In the mid nineteenth century, following the Disruption of 1843, the new Free Church of Scotland built its theological college, known today as New College, on the site and some years later added an Assembly Hall within the college premises. In 1929, the year which saw the final coming back together of much of Scotland's fragmented presbyterianism, the reunited Church of Scotland chose to hold its annual gatherings in the New

College Assembly Hall rather than the Highland Tolbooth Church on Castlehill (now the Edinburgh Festival "Hub") where the pre-union Church of Scotland Assembly had met. From 1999 until 2004 the 'reconvened' Scottish Parliament met in the Kirk's Assembly Hall before moving into the new parliament building at Holyrood.

The Assembly Hall has been home to memorable debates over the years. There was a time in the mid twentieth century when the General Assembly was regarded as the nearest thing Scotland had to a parliament. Those who attended had no democratic mandate, but they came from parishes around Scotland, from the highlands and the lowlands, from great cities and sparsely populated islands - ministers and elders, people very much in touch with their local communities – and there, gathered in the General Assembly Hall, they debated great issues affecting church and nation. These included nuclear disarmament, the case for political devolution, the question of whether repentance could allow a murderer to become a minister, abortion (with an elder who had undergone an abortion speaking in the debate) and the ordination of women – to mention just a few.

Protest groups were also regularly attracted to Mound Place in front of the Assembly Hall - perhaps most famously, the late Pastor Jack Glass, who fulminated against ecumenical initiatives, particularly those involving the Roman Catholic Church. However, such protests did not prevent another great moment in the Hall's history when in June 1982 the Moderator, Professor John McIntyre, received Pope John Paul II and welcomed him on behalf of Scotland's national church.

In the late 19th century the self same Hall echoed to great theological debates over the authority and interpretation of Scripture, with people queuing for hours, Wimbledon style, to have a ringside seat for heresy trials of people such as William Robertson Smith. His scholarship, which subjected the sacred texts of the Bible to the scrutiny of literary criticism, was making the religious establishment of the day nervous. Removed from his chair in Aberdeen he was soon appointed to another in Cambridge. Even as recently as 2006 there were queues to gain access to the public gallery for a General Assembly debate on whether to authorise ministers to bless civil partnerships.

There had been quite a build up to the 2011 Assembly, with speculation about another Disruption like that of 1843. That year one-third of the General Assembly had walked out over issues to do with the spiritual freedom of the Church and formed the Free Church of Scotland. The 2009 General Assembly had allowed an openly gay minister in a civil partnership to be inducted to a congregation but then gone on to remit the whole question of same sex relationships and the ministry to a Special Commission. This Commission was instructed to report in 2011 and the expectation was that that year's Assembly would have to make decisions which, whatever those decisions were, could result in a significant loss of ministers and members.

With all this in mind the Assembly business managers had prudently set aside a whole day for the debate and so on Monday 23rd May Luke, along with several hundred others took their places in the Assembly Hall with a sense of occasion and of the considerable responsibilities laid upon them.

The Monday of Assembly week traditionally begins with a service of Holy Communion. Luke found himself sitting beside a fellow minister whom he knew by reputation but had not previously met. This minister was a leading light in the conservative wing of the Church and was strongly opposed to the admission of sexually active gay people into the ministry. Luke recalled reading something he had written in *Ministers' Forum*, an in-house magazine circulated monthly to ministers. This article was along the lines of having no difficulty with a gay minister who was celibate. However, homosexual acts, even within a legal civil partnership were always sinful. His reading of the Bible, the writer maintained, left him unable to come to any other view.

Luke introduced himself and the two men chatted pleasantly as they waited for the communion service to begin. They talked about their parishes, their families, holiday plans, mutual acquaintances - everything under the sun except the business of the day – and a very congenial conversation it was. Based on what he had heard his neighbour say in the past and his reading of his articles Luke had formed a rather negative view of this individual. He had come across to Luke as quite harsh and judgmental but, face to face, he proved to be a most interesting and engaging conversationalist. Judge not, that ye be not judged thought Luke, in a mild rebuke to himself.

At this point the Assembly officer appeared and proclaimed "Moderator." Everyone stood and the Moderator called the Assembly to worship. The next moment the hall reverberated to a thousand voices singing *Ye gates lift up your heads on high* to the tune St George's Edinburgh – verses from Psalm 24 traditionally used in the Church of Scotland communion service. And so the service proceeded with the sharing of bread and wine, recalling Christ's last supper with his original disciples and affirming his presence with his disciples today. Then, before the closing hymn a pause where people were invited to shake hands with those around them, look them in the eye and say "the peace of Christ be with you." So Luke turned to his new friend and they shared the peace as invited, each naming the other as they spoke the words. And Luke thought, "I mean it. We shall probably vote in different ways later, but for now we are at one, at peace and equally sincere in our Christian faith and convictions. Whatever this day brings this is a good moment."

And then it was time to begin the debate.

The Moderator prefaced this with a plea for courtesy and consideration and a reminder that, while the matter before the Assembly was one on which strong and divergent views were held, there were many more matters on which members of the Assembly were agreed. There should be no "them and us" he asserted, "only us." This was greeted with warm approval.

The Convener of the Special Commission spoke to the report and took a number of questions. It was then time to move to the debate proper.

A preliminary skirmish ensued over the question of what constituted homophobia. The Commission wanted the Assembly to declare homophobia to be "sinful," but then went on to exclude from the definition of homophobia "the *bona fide* belief that homosexual practice is contrary to God's will and the responsible statement of that belief in preaching or writing."

Luke had spotted this as an attempt to accommodate the range of opinion within the Assembly and keep everyone on board as far as possible. However, someone proposed that the qualification be removed, fearing that the word "responsible" would be interpreted in widely differing ways. However, the Assembly, acknowledging the strength of feeling of those who genuinely believed that homosexual practice was wrong, voted to retain the qualification.

The next big test arose over a recommendation that ministers in same sex relationships, who had been ordained before the moratorium imposed by the 2009 Assembly, should be free to be inducted to pastoral charges. The Commission's view was that this was simply safeguarding the position of those individuals who were most directly affected by the current debate. However, others saw this variously as the thin end of a wedge, a Trojan horse, or a selling of the pass before any final decisions had been made. After several speeches the matter was put to a vote and the Commission's proposal was approved by 393 votes to 252 against. This resulted in over 100 members entering their dissent.

If the earlier vote on what constituted homophobia appeared to be a victory for the conservative/traditionalist wing this decision now looked like a win for the revisionist/progressive side of the argument.

The next significant amendment proposed was to the effect that the Assembly should not be asked to give a steer to the new Theological Commission. The argument for this was that, having decided that more work needed to be done it seemed premature to narrow the scope of that work to just one side of the argument. Surely it would be better for the Theological Commission to have as wide a remit as possible and then come back in 2013 with proposals one way or the other.

There was strong support within the Assembly for this attempt to find a middle way but, the majority clearly felt it was a fudge. Their argument was that the Church expected some kind of decision to be made and the Assembly should have the courage to make it. This view prevailed and the delaying amendment was defeated by 347 votes to 303. Some commentators afterwards thought that both parties were emboldened by their earlier successes to believe that they could carry the day. Certainly Luke had voted against what he thought was a fudge. The unity of the Church was something to be prized highly, but at what price, he wondered? Was it at the price of rejecting people like Ailsa and Mary White and her daughter, not to mention those ministers who had shared their stories of pain and rejection with the Special Commission?

This set the stage for a final debate between steering the Theological Commission in the direction of imposing a permanent moratorium on the ordination of practising homosexual ministers or contemplating the removal of the current holding moratorium altogether. It was for this point that Luke had prepared a speech in support of what he saw as the more enabling option, namely the potential lifting of the moratorium and exploration of whether the commitment expressed in civil partnerships might carry some equivalence to the commitment represented by marriage. Some six hours into the debate, with many people still indicating a desire to speak, Luke was beginning to think that his chances of being called were pretty slim. Then, suddenly, he heard the Moderator call his name: "The Reverend Luke Paul."

I'm on, thought Luke as he made his way to the microphone. He had spoken on a few occasions in previous General Assemblies, but it's not the sort of thing you get used to. Luke had observed the various moods of the General Assembly. A clearly nervous commissioner making a faltering maiden speech will be heard with great courtesy. By contrast the seasoned and eloquent Assembly goer offering his fourth contribution in the course of a day can find himself approaching the microphone to the sound of mutters and grumbles. Luke knew that people would be getting tired and that his contribution should be succinct and to the point. He had timed his speech at four minutes. Speakers were allowed five but a bell went after four to indicate it was time to wind up. He had observed people gabbling through that final minute to complete what they had prepared. Big mistake, Luke thought. Better to finish before the "turn off" effect of the bell on the audience.

This is what he said:

Moderator, there was a time when I would have been opposed to the prospect of the ministry being open to practising homosexual individuals, but my years in parish ministry have led me to re-think a number of opinions I held when I started out. I dare to suggest that others of my vintage in the Assembly could say the same.

We have come a fair distance on this subject in recent years and have now reached a point where those on both sides of the argument acknowledge that the other side is equally sincere in seeking to interpret what the Bible says. Today, I suggest, it is easier for those of us who are sympathetic to openly gay ministers in the Church to stand here and say so than it would have been twenty years ago. And that isn't a case of caving in to social pressures; rather, it's through becoming more informed about the genetics and biology which determines who and what we are. I find it significant that an overwhelming majority of those who responded to the consultation believe that our sexuality is a given, not a choice. Again, I wonder what the response would have been twenty years ago. Opinion is shifting as we become better informed and knowledge challenges prejudice.

Last year we marked the 450th anniversary of the Scottish Reformation and that is an important part of our inheritance. This year sees the 300th anniversary of the birth of David Hume – perhaps not the most obvious individual for the Church of Scotland to commemorate. Yet the movement of which he was part along with prominent ministers of the day, the Scottish Enlightenment, is also included in our heritage. Since the eighteenth century the Church has faced divisions over what was then described as new and old light thinking. We affirm the Word of God contained in the Bible but I suggest we can also see the discoveries of science as God given revelations, shedding new light on our understanding of the human condition and the world around us. In this connection I particularly thank the Special Commission for the background papers outlining the insights of genetic and biological research in the area of sexuality.

In the lifetime of many here the Church has embraced new thinking on questions such as the re-marriage of divorced persons in church and the ordination of women to the ministry and eldership – to take just two examples. I believe the issue before us today is but the latest old light-new light challenge to face the Church and I urge the Assembly to support the more progressive of the two options before us. This way we shall keep open the possibility of accepting homosexual individuals into the ministry, subject to equivalent constraints on sexual conduct as are placed upon heterosexual ministers.

There is one more thing I would like to say, Moderator. When my own Kirk Session discussed the matter there were those who were opposed and those who were open to the prospect of openly gay ministers. No surprise there. But one contribution particularly sticks in my mind. It was from an elder who was not personally happy with the idea but did not believe that the matter was so fundamental as to force him out of the Church if the decision went against his feelings. We have heard a great deal in recent months about a split in the Church similar to the Disruption. I hope and pray that it will not come to that but that we will be able to find a way of containing our differences on this, as on other matters, within the unity of our broad church.

When the final vote was taken it turned out that Luke had backed the successful motion. Whether his speech had persuaded some who might not have voted that way will never be known. As anticipated the vote was close, but also quite clear with 351 voting in favour of the Theological Commission focussing on issues which would need to be addressed were the Church to accept to openly gay ministers and 294 voting in support of the contrary focus, namely, the implications of a decision to impose a permanent moratorium on such acceptance. Of those voting with the minority 76 asked that their dissent be recorded.

The following day the debate was prominently reported in the newspapers, with one national journal quoting part of Luke's speech. When Joyce drew this to his attention he was both pleased and anxious. Remembering that on a previous occasion media coverage had prompted some members of his congregation to leave he wondered if history might be about the repeat itself. And then, a couple of night's later, BBC Scotland's Assembly round-up programme featured the debate and there he was again - Luke on screen for all who wished to see and hear.

Later that evening Richard phoned. "I saw you on the telly earlier, Dad. I'm still not persuaded and I think your plea for people not to leave the Church is a pretty hopeless cause. Already I've had another half dozen people cancelling their standing orders and talking of leaving. I've tried to explain that we haven't reached the end of the road. More work is being done and it will be 2013 before we have a final decision. But they're not interested. They say it's clear which way things are going and that our credibility is shot through."

"I'm sorry to hear that, "said Luke, quite genuinely. "What about your own position, Richard? And what does Alison think?"

"We'll take stock," Richard replied. "While perhaps it's a vain hope you may well be right about this not being a resigning issue. And anyway, I'm too thirled to the Kirk, for good or ill. It must be in the genes! So just let's wait and see what happens in 2013."

The following evening it was Anne's turn.

"Hi dad, Archie and I were out last night but we recorded the Assembly report and have just watched it. That was quite a speech you made. We're both very proud of you. It couldn't have been easy and Mum told me about the civil partnership you blessed as well. My, you are living dangerously in your old age."

"Enough of that," said Luke. "I'll 'old age' you, but I appreciate your support."

"Any reaction in the parish?" asked Anne.

"Not so far, but I have a Session meeting next week so there may be something there."

In fact Luke didn't have to wait that long. The following morning's post brought letters from Peter Henderson and Jimmy Souter resigning from the Kirk Session. Peter indicated that he was moving to a neighbouring congregation where the minister's views were more in keeping with his own. Coincidentally, Luke had discovered that this minister was one of those who had complained about his blessing of Ailsa's and Liz's civil partnership. He had also been making noises about leaving the Church of Scotland altogether over the matter and possibly taking his congregation with him. Meanwhile Jimmy's letter stated simply that he was taking a break from church going until this whole thing was settled. Then he would decide, in light of what was finally agreed whether or not to "return to the fold" (as he put it).

Luke was not surprised. There had been something of an atmosphere around his relationship with Peter and Jimmy since that morning in his study last winter when they expressed their unhappiness over his blessing a civil partnership. His Assembly speech was probably the final straw. Still, he was vexed that this time they had not come to see him, either separately or together as on the previous occasion. In replying to their letters he would ask if he could call on them, not to try to change their minds, but to thank them for all they had done in Capelaw and to wish them well for the future.

But now, as Richard had put it, it was "wait and see time." In the weeks following the Assembly there were reports of ministers and congregations leaving the Church of Scotland over the Assembly's decision. In response to these reports were calls from Church officials not to pre-judge the outcome of the Theological Commission's work which would come to the General Assembly of 2013. It was most unlikely that Luke would be a commissioner to that Assembly and there was a part of him which said, "for this relief much thanks." In any event he was due to retire that year and was content to have had his say on the subject. Meantime there was work to be done in these remaining years of his ministry and it would be good to return to that without the strains and stresses occasioned by this past year's debate.

Luke often thought back to that momentous debate on 23 May 2011 and the fact that he had spoken in it. But what he particularly recalled was that he had enjoyed friendly conversation and shared Christ's peace with a fellow minister who took an entirely contrary view of the matter. Looking to the future his hope and prayer remained that those who disagreed might yet remain within the one Church of Scotland and work together in a spirit of Christian peace and unity.

After all, he thought, Luke and Paul were very different people but the richness of the Christian Gospel owes much to them both.